I0843441

BACK-STABBING
NEUROTICS
KAREN
KELLOCK

BACKSTABBING NEUROTICS

Karen Kellock Ph.D.

Manual for
Superior Men

This is a complete theory based on Einstein physics,
Political Psychology, Systems Theory
and Archetypal Psychiatry.

FORMULA

All success attraction
All disease obstruction
All recovery elimination

You must fast on all three

OBSTRUCTIONS:

People
Habit
Food

BACKSTABBING NEUROTICS

An evil helper is a backstabbing witch. She feigns helpfulness just to destroy you sis.   Sorry to tell you this but the world's an evil place and you must be on the defense: get a fence.   You see the truth about relationship when differences crop up for they threaten a narcissist who can't meet you in the middle--justifying anger, smear campaigns and bullying creating more trouble.

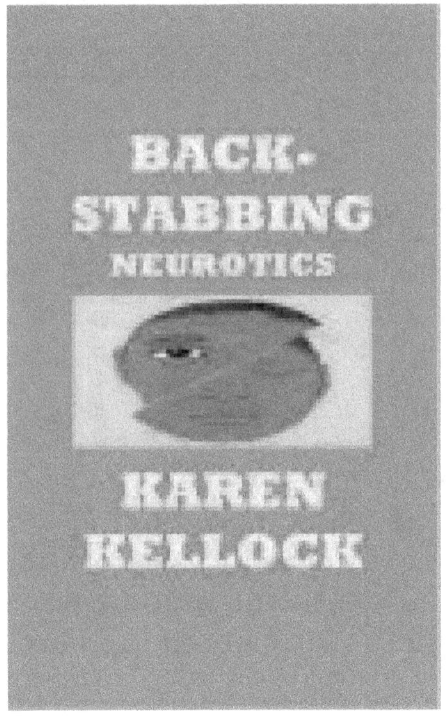

OVERCOMING BACKSTABBERS

DON'T EVER HAVE AN AFFAIR
ALCOHOL THE MORAL DISINHIBITOR
TRUST PEOPLE UNTIL YOU CAN'T
THE BENEFITS FROM LOST LOVE
MAKING GOLD AFTER A CRASH
KEEP HAPPY THOUGHTS FOR MIRACLES
NEED CARBS FOR ENERGY, BUT...
FINALLY FOUND THE RIGHT DIET

OVERCOMING BACKSTABBERS

DON'T EVER HAVE AN AFFAIR

Whatever you do, never have an affair. It ruins your life forever as it's against God not just the other.

Even if it happens "just once" it's hard to pull out and the other gets vindictive and confronts.

One must have hard unbreakable moral guidelines for this is a demon ready to trigger you, aye.

You can have everything going for you but I promise this demon will bring it all down in a minute too.

Alcohol is the trigger the devil uses to start an affair that seems innocent at first while you take the dare.

ALCOHOL THE MORAL DISINHIBITOR

Alcohol is the lubricant to melt down morals. It's a moral disinhibitor and suddenly life topples.

It happens in a blackout--you're really not responsible--but your spouse won't care, it's all over doll.

The house, the cars, the in-laws, even career can topple in a minute by an affair starting so "innocent".

Staunch morality saves your happy life but it all implodes quickly if morals are taken frivolously.

So you live in a mansion with money to burn. This can all turn around suddenly if to others you turn.

Acting irrationally has real life consequences. Guard your life constantly or you're up a creek miss.

OVERCOMING BACKSTABBERS

She who smashed car windows/painted "cheat" on the side was arrested for felony vandalism, aye.

TRUST PEOPLE UNTIL YOU CAN'T

I know you've been burned but trust people til you can't. Commit em to God & He'll use em as promised.

Don't keep riding one you've paid to do the work. Commit em to God and don't be a jerk.

Begin your day cosmically. That's being ready for a sudden change beyond your wildest dreams see.

Don't ever rise to another humdrum day. Never see it that way for with God things happen SUDDENLY.

As Jung said, "watch for miracles like a cat watches a mousehole." That's the way to live if whole.

Things speed up in times of transition. Watch for magic synchronicity as it all comes together son.

THE BENEFITS FROM LOST LOVE

That one who was a wrecking ball of your life actually saved you as you found your Self, aye.

That beloved being was just fleeting and a catalyst that shattered the walls you're now releasing.

Lost love sets off irreversible transformation. It's not meant to stay but to tear your apart son.

Lost love plunged you into darkness where true growth happens. Illusions were gone, from devastation.

Lost love burned off the dead weight keeping you bound to an old version of self, entirely unsound.

OVERCOMING BACKSTABBERS

Look at the gold after you've healed. Your soul was scraped down and rebuilt into warm steel.

Your fractured aching heart was pieced back together not by another but your own will, like a mother.

You pulled your innocent child from neglect & bathed in the nurturance it always deserved as an Elect.

Those chains no more hold you captive & those scars are symbols of the battle making you attractive.

You're now grounded in a way inconceivable before. The storms gave roots like a mountain adored.

MAKING GOLD AFTER A CRASH

You now have a shining CENTER that is only possible from surviving your own personal hell sister.

Through this grounding you've made gold, unlocking a much higher version of yourself and BOLD.

You've now stepped into your own light, the one that has always been there waiting so bright.

Your heart is now open, not to anyone else but the vast potential of YOU, a result of that connection.

That past connection was never about them but about you, the chosen one. It had to happen son.

The fire they sparked in you burned away all illusions, the kid stuff keeping you bound and down.

It left your truest & most powerful self standing in the ash. It had to happen: making gold from a crash.

Now you rise. Look at you: standing stronger than ever, a rare diamond shining so elegant and bright.

OVERCOMING BACKSTABBERS

Forged by fires the foes thought would break you: They can't imagine how you survived after the screw.

You're now a force to be reckoned with. You're now unshakable and unmovable like a megalith.

KEEP HAPPY THOUGHTS FOR MIRACLES

Hope for the best, expect the worst. That's the way some end up after going through this curse.

The cosmic flow is there for you to know. You have only to become available by knowing about it now.

Sometimes you get in the cosmic flow not by urgently working but just by laying down and thinking.

You're most apt to be part of by relaxing. Access it just by knowing it's there: miracle in the making.

To become part of this miraculous adventure don't let negative thoughts take over. Be more clever.

Bad memories are there to do Satan's work: to block you forever from doing God's work first.

Don't let em come up or block em when they do. You have much to attend to with miracles too.

Envision Satan sitting on your shoulder reminding you of your faults and embarrassing encounters.

Block em, block em, block em. Keep only happy thoughts all day for miracles to come in.

Have glorified thoughts of the future not apprehensive thoughts of the past, and you're there at last.

If destined for greatness be bound to God's seasons. A season of planting, waiting then harvesting son.

OVERCOMING BACKSTABBERS

NEED CARBS FOR ENERGY, BUT...

Adding fruit to the lowcarb diet I felt so immeasurably better, it was like a light flipping on, a glare!

Ehret said: "fruits–fresh or canned". They're canned at the peak of ripeness and they keep so buy it.

Who doesn't want their digestive-eliminative to work perfectly? That's the best part actually.

The lowcarb flue is from suddenly withdrawing carbs which give us energy. Never again I say.

Sure you will lose weight and sure the body will switch to burning fat but it's still not superiority.

Fruits & vegetables, fruits & vegetables: that's the mean thing to get in your head or be fat/die instead.

Protein? But low-protein [poor] cultures lived long, healthy and energetic lives. So why all the hype?

Why are athletes & marathon runners all on high carb diets? That alone should tell us to like it.

But you don't have to eat truckloads of fruit. Fat collapses calories so we can have that too.

Don't be afraid of fruit sugar & don't be afraid of fat. Fear processed starches and things like that.

Fruitarian-starchivores tell us to avoid all fat. They look "bready", fatarians look sleek: think of that.

FINALLY FOUND THE RIGHT DIET

We don't just need carbs or calories for energy, for they're low in veggies. It's the micronutrients see!

OVERCOMING BACKSTABBERS

When I took vegetables I felt energy at a whole new level. I couldn't believe how good I felt.

Athletes who rely on sugar in processed carbs are missing out if they don't take the veggies sir.

Veggies are low in calories, carbs and fat--but high in fiber & the great micronutrients and all of that.

I switched salads & cooked veg with cheese for processed starches and what a refreshing breeze!

NOW I started to lose the weight. I slimmed right down with delicious salads & veggies on my plate.

Boatloads of fruit? Hell no. Fruit yes but the salads and veggies are the main course you know.

I felt so good I felt I could run up a mountain. All with low calories or carbs they said I'd need, amen.

If I need calories then a little cheese adds em in. Protein too if we really need that to begin.

After going thru all diets written of by man, I've finally found it feeling better than when I began.

I didn't lose weight with loads of fruits & starches. You can have "raw til 4", the old path is the skinny door.

SUFFERING OR TRANSFORMATION

KNOW WHAT YOU'RE BEEN THROUGH
HURTS PREPARE YOU FOR THE FUTURE
GUILT IS USED BY THE ENEMY
YOUR WALLS ARE NOT SELFISHNESS
GOD GAVE YOU DISCERNMENT
SICK OF BAD ATTRACTIONS
FINDING TRUE SELF AFTER THEY'RE GONE
TAKE YOUR R & R VERY SERIOUSLY
FRUIT, FAT AND FASTING [CHAMPION GUIDES]
THOSE PROCESSED STARCHES
HIGH FAT IS WHERE IT'S AT
ADD CHEESE TO BROCCOLI
FOCUS ON MICRONUTRIENTS
ALMOND BUTTER AND FRUIT
THEY PUT DOWN FATS AND OILS

SUFFERING OR TRANSFORMATION

KNOW WHAT YOU'RE BEEN THROUGH

They woulda been dead by now with similar obstacles. But yet they're still envious, that's the peoples.

You were in the excruciating fire to strip away the dross and it hurt like "hell" to make you the boss.

What others call "suffering" you now know as transformation. In other words, it all had to happen.

Success is a testament that you faced what shoulda destroyed you but you got strong from it.

You're trained to bear burdens they can't even grasp. They have no idea your painful path to success.

HURTS PREPARE YOU FOR THE FUTURE

Those challenges prepared you for a future far greater than they can comprehend, that's it friend.

Each obstacle overcome equipped you to withstand something the others never could or can.

You must KNOW these things about yourself so when envy arises you know what it's all about.

The sleepless nights when false accusation and insinuation made you grey: that's the fight.

Knowing your historical differences will build you up when jealousy rears up so now just look up.

Chosen ones are constantly challenged to keep spiritual energy elevated: don't answer phones I said.

SUFFERING OR TRANSFORMATION

They must protect their mind and heart from negative influences. This constant battle is promised.

Every phone call is an opportunity to strengthen or weaken your energy. Remember that please.

If you feel drained, exhausted or troubled after a call it's spiritual exhaustion: see it as a sign that's all.

Connect with people who energize & uplift you while firmly setting boundaries with darkness too.

GUILT IS USED BY THE ENEMY

Guilt is used by the enemy to make you question your decisions. Be firm I say and just don't listen.

Do you answer calls so you don't seem rude? Even worse, do you let em in like that crazy dude?

Satan makes us feel obligated to always be available & accessible but this is pure unadulterated bull.

They act like ignoring a call is a flaw in your character. But protected your light & strength is a must sir.

Learn to say NO and trust this decision is guided by God. Don't ever feel guilty--get over this flaw.

Setting boundaries tells the world & enemy your mission is sacred. It's admirable to be self-protected.

YOUR WALLS ARE NOT SELFISHNESS

Your walls are NOT selfishness or pride but divine protections or your spirit fills with strife.

You must continue your work as a chosen one without constantly being interrupted or diverted hon'.

SUFFERING OR TRANSFORMATION

The constant calls are more than interruptions but demonic weapons to undermine your work son.

Satan wants to weaken your connection to the divine and constant calls surely does that, aye.

Every time you refuse a call you strengthen your spiritual armor so take pride in your silence sir.

You must take pride in your gifts and help your spiritual journey by heeding these tips & staying free.

Those calls you choose to ignore or answer are choices influencing your spiritual state: low or great.

GOD GAVE YOU DISCERNMENT

God has given you a gift of discernment precisely to make decisions in this busy world flooding in.

Not all voices deserve your attention, not all invites are meant to be accepted. This is God's edict.

Don't let distractions infiltrate your life. That is the road to success: making constant choices, aye.

Close all doors that don't build you up. it's as simple as that: it's not selfish it's God's destiny: fact.

It was no accident they seared into your life. It was meant to trigger impulses/shatter illusions, aye.

God was demanding you confront the truth. WHY were you attracted, was is a primal urge [uncouth]?

You felt the undeniable pull, went with it and got hurt. That the lesson you learned, removing a curse.

SICK OF BAD ATTRACTIONS

SUFFERING OR TRANSFORMATION

Hitting the wall with bad attractions is where transformation begins, a need since birth friend.

They were sent to unmake you and strip away all your false identities, pretenses and defenses.

They came in with a splash so sudden it ignited a fire burning within bringing out all things hidden.

Their energy consumed you, sinking into your very essence. It was a trip by their mere presence.

They triggered the dormant, buried parts of your psyche waiting for an awakening, I recall it darling.

They laid bare the traumas you'd hidden away, the unresolved conflicts deadening night and day.

It's a big reason to guard your children & watch who they befriend for life changes suddenly, amen.

FINDING TRUE SELF AFTER THEY'RE GONE

After the explosion came the breaking point of silence. It was a collapse, a star dissolving to nothingness.

They left a black hole sucking the life out of everything. That's how it happens while you're evolving.

Through that void and the desolation they left behind you found your SELF and what a rare find!

You had to go with your desires to back out suddenly and change forever, choosing godly purity.

When love was lost there was nothing to do but face vacuity then return to the true self & destiny.

Returning to your first nature is such a relief, free of all shackles and delusions from the energy thief.

SUFFERING OR TRANSFORMATION

The lost love blasted your second nature apart then left you to pick up the pieces: your true self, a star.

When left with nothing but a dry desert, God turned it into fertile land with the talents inborn.

To be left with nothing, God had most to work with by simply turning on the switch you were born with.

It happened to me in a tiny cabin in a desert wilderness: suddenly seeing how much I had to work with.

TAKE YOUR R & R VERY SERIOUSLY

See your R & R as necessary to improve your work. Take it as seriously as diligent effort or be cursed.

ATTACK unhappy memories. You must see them as little gremlins who just wanna bring you down see.

God wants you to be happy: that means R & R, enjoying & loving your work and attacking unhappy memory.

You must take your R & R more seriously, for that alone fuels your passion for work and creativity.

Work, don't work. Eat, don't eat. There are two speeds to life like work days and the end of the week.

I for one couldn't stop working. There was always that approval neurosis egging me on while losing.

Letting attention and focus DOWN is what makes that great insight and revelation arise UP: wow.

After enough R & R you shouldn't work unless CALLED to it: to be drawn like a magnet to attack it.

WAIT until called to work. It's a CLICK in your head when all you wanna do is immerse yourself instead.

SUFFERING OR TRANSFORMATION

Relax, for your work and destiny is a divine MIRACLE so it should be easy: with holy spirit ease see.

There will be no more embarrassment over self, since relaxation disperses attention out & way off.

You can have unbelievable wealth that is overshadowed by familial discord and tragedy, becoming hell.

Your miseries shaped you. Your invaders made you who you are today, well-fortified and splendid too.

Imagine the stress reduction from facing eviction and then getting a rent-free mansion. It's God man.

FRUIT, FAT AND FASTING [CHAMPION GUIDES]

I don't see it as fasting, cuz after I eat one meal, before i know it the day is over & I'm not hungry ever.

Fruit, fat and fasting. Salsa, lowcarb veggies, cheese, olive oil, lettuce, nutbutters: fats and skinny.

No meat nor starch, it slows me down too much. Just cheese/fish/fruit w/out bread/pasta as such.

Read my Champion Guides for the correct diet: fruit, fat and fasting. You won't be hungry, count on it.

This a.m. I had lettuce, salsa, melted cheese and shrimp with parmesan and that's all for the day friends.

I eat before dawn, like a Ramadan fast. That way the day is for miracles and having a total blast.

THOSE PROCESSED STARCHES

Processed starches like pasta, noodles or tortillas ruined the skinny trip I'm on, I'm not kidding ya.

SUFFERING OR TRANSFORMATION

People don't know what they're doing when shopping. There's no integrating paradigm on planning.

Just buy fruit, tomatoes, cilantro, green onions, lowcarb veg, cheese and shrimp: that'll do it.

It's lacto-fruitarian, also rasta [fish]. That's enough for any palette craving flavor and a delicious dish.

Non-sweet fruits are tomato, zuchini, yellow squash, peppers. Anything with seed is fruit for sure.

I thought I could do spaghetti or noodles if eating just once a day. I couldn't, it didn't work that way.

HIGH FAT IS WHERE IT'S AT

After a high-fat meal like that there's no hunger for 24 hours. If you must, have a tab of nut-butter.

With starches or meat I looked rough. Too round & ill-defined: as an artist I saw it was the wrong stuff.

Fruit and cheese, tomato salsas, lettuce and fish please. How very European don't you think?

I tried regular low carb. I was STARVED for the fruits which instantly gave me an energetic charge.

Eliminating processed starches and the meat will be enough to lose the weight and lift you up.

Eliminating all sugary treats and just keeping the fruits will be enough to satisfy your sweet tooth.

Best of all on the KK diet your can keep the healthy fats: good oils, avocado, nutbutters and tallow.

ADD CHEESE TO BROCCOLI

SUFFERING OR TRANSFORMATION

You can add cheese to your broccoli and parmesan on your salads and be satisfied: it's all valid.

Call it lacto-fruitarian but also rasta [fish]-vegetarian. It's extremely healthy and of so European.

I tried lowcarb and all I dreamed about was refreshing pineapple which is high in carbs ya know.

I thought it was lowcarb flue when I was so tired for weeks. I ate my pineapple and no more fatigue.

The fruit and fat diet is combined with fasting. It's no problem since aren't hungry all day see.

FOCUS ON MICRONUTRIENTS

I focused on getting micronutrients from broccoli for example. Fry with cheese, for a meal it's ample.

It's God's food: fruits, veggies with cheese & fish on the side. You'll be so healthy [Champion Guides].

You won't care about the backstabbing neurotics anymore. You'll be so high, to hell with the whore.

I was SO relieved to add the sweet fruits to my diet. I'll never go lowcarb again, read CG and apply it.

Even the "Animal Diet" is half fruit: fruit & meat together are essential and primal with energy to boot.

I tried the fruit diet with starches [raw til 4: rice or noodles at night]. No way, that too wasn't right.

On the lowcarb diet I cried out to God: WHY did I feel so fatigued including this awful brain fog?

ALMOND BUTTER AND FRUIT

SUFFERING OR TRANSFORMATION

I returned to my breakfast of almond butter & pineapple chunks, praising God for my good luck.

Drop all your ingrained paranoia over healthy fats and sugary fruits. God made em and you'll be cute.

Lacto-fruitarian, that's where it's at man. The land of milk and honey or pomegranates and dairy.

Brain fog: I need fruits to lighten my load, illuminate my way and erase fatigue/shoot up my energy.

Check out the fruit & starch crowd. They look rough in their forties [the true test]: you'll be appalled.

THEY PUT DOWN FATS AND OILS

They put down fats and oils as fattening while lowcarbers put down fruits: ignore all the babbling.

The starchivores while thin look pale and washed out. This isn't the true diet, it doesn't have clout.

But on my diet you can have corn, peas and spuds: these are real things God made, not duds.

I love yellow corn in stewed tomatoes, even tho' it has dreaded sugar in it. Who cares? Go for it.

Try my diet and throw all their theories out the window and take on mine which is true ya know.

MODERN TOXICITY

MODERN TOXICITY HURTS LIKE HELL
END TIMES TERROR
SINS OF THE LATTER DAYS
EVERYONE'S SELFISH
FACE REALITY: NO ONE CARES
SOCIAL DESPERATION TURNOFF
SHAME IS PUT *ON* US
THE SHAME MONSTER
LATE LIFE ANOREXIA
SISTER ABUSE
AFTER THE DARK IS LIGHT
BY NOT BEING STRAIGHT
THE FASTING EDICT FOR SUCCESS
SEE IT AS A SPECIAL DAY
DESIGNATE FOODS

MODERN TOXICITY

MODERN TOXICITY HURTS LIKE HELL

The modern world has become so toxic that intuitive people would rather be alone, believe it.

People want friends to benefit them and they don't care beyond that: that's quite an insight lad.

They lack so much anyway: people are empty these days and they just won't be around ok.

Intuitive empaths will prefer being around animals who seem real, lovable and predictable.

They are not what they proposed to be so how can they be a solid friend? It's nonexistent.

They act like they like you and even say they love you then in a few days they ghost you.

Prophetically the latter days would show people rising up and suddenly hating each other ok.

His mask slipped and you saw who he was. Tho' married for 20 years you were lost in a fog.

END TIMES TERROR

The end times: humans increasingly distant from God. Famines, earthquakes and hate by the flawed.

In these times people are scandalized and hate one another. Is addiction into death any wonder?

As evil increases, love of many weakens Not by chance, Jesus said at the end it would happen.

MODERN TOXICITY

Men would be selfish, covetous, boastful, arrogant, disrespectful, ungrateful and perverse.

Men would become slanderers and irreconcilable. You can't resolve these conflicts which double.

Men lose all self-control and become cruel haters of good. Everything you say is misunderstood.

Husbands would become reckless traitors and proud lovers of pleasure--you see it everywhere.

Husbands having forms of godliness but denying its power: never seeking God while falling lower.

No one's better at self-deception than men who batter women. This is happening all over, amen.

They seek new relationships to find other women to batter. They carry this need within sir.

While eating potato chips & dip he treated her like shit. Meanwhile she was scared to report it.

One in three marriages in the U.S. involve some form of physical abuse. Has this affected you too?

SINS OF THE LATTER DAYS

We're only here for a brief while then we're gone. We have to suffer evil for a time & rely on God.

The first sin to Paul was selfishness. You see it on social media where we're all full of ourselves.

Selfishness kills the essence of man cuz it separates him from God. Loving God & neighbor is gone.

What I learned in Psalms is: we can't rely on human comfort. Just when in need, it exits.

MODERN TOXICITY

Human love is flaky, frail and faulty. What I've learned in all emergencies is to rely on God/the godly.

Why fear returned: After realizing God's love & protection she merged with husband again.

Immorality and unholiness is a sin dominating the entire world. Sex sin is against your own body girl.

Once there is values-conflict in the relationship it's over. They won't care about you now or ever.

EVERYONE'S SELFISH

Unless you give em money, everyone's selfish. it's a scary thing in the latter days: devilish.

Your friendship only exists if it serves them: makes me feel more empowered or gives value friend.

Even "caring" people are boosting their image of being caring persons: they're virtue signaling.

True saints are few. Don't kid yourself about caring people, everyone's boosting their image dude.

Big corporations give to charity cuz it makes em look better, to hide all they're doing undercover.

In your interactions with others, remember it's just a facade that they care about you brother.

Selfishness is number one sin of latter days and it's one reason alcoholism is the biggest malaise.

FACE REALITY: NO ONE CARES

They don't have your best interest at heart. 95% of it is B.S. and to be safe you gotta see this sis.

MODERN TOXICITY

People care less about you than you think. They wanna "promote your book" but it's all rinky-dink.

Knowing these things about people gives you freedom & distance so you won't appear so dumb sis.

What other people are throwing you is just to use you. They don't really care so get a grip Sue.

It makes you happier cuz you don't have to work so hard to maintain pseudo-friendships [all B.S.].

Most want to believe people care so they can live in la-la land but the result is dire: life is bland.

SOCIAL DESPERATION TURNOFF

Don't ever tell em how "desperately you need friends" cuz they'll reject you even more, amen.

Van Gogh cut off his ear when Gauguin left him. He was happy when painting, this was after drinkin'.

Desperation over friends is wrong thinking. We're joyous in the right brain just doing our thing.

Ground yourself in your own values. What you truly care about: just your own life & talents dude.

The best way to contribute to the world is to first help yourself so YOU are the contribution itself.

Money, recognition and power: these are the three things motivating us humans forever.

As evil increases in the latter days the love of many weakens, that's a promise & obvious guys.

SHAME IS PUT *ON* US

MODERN TOXICITY

Don't fret immature mistakes you've made. They're all dead or the living ones will forget it instead.

God is NOT all-loving. He hates our enemies. If you don't believe me read the Psalms please.

Shame is a prison. Every time you feel it you feed the shame monster with less reason for livin'.

Don't feed shame for it only increases your pain so send it back to hell from whence it came.

Shame was put on you to lower your self-image. It's toxic and part of a sick system marriage.

Shame erodes your self-esteem so every thought you have about yourself is colored by it see.

If infected with shame every thought about yourself is embarrassing. You must fight this thing.

THE SHAME MONSTER

Shame is a monster you're feeding continuously until it gets so massive you'd just like to die.

From what the Psalms says after full repentance of sins you may expect a reprieve/reward friends.

When fear returns, take a look at your repentance of sins and know it's all irrational, you'll win.

If one repents of sins he can count on escaping traps & being rewarded with success & all that.

You read Psalms & feel assured. When old fears return you know it's not real cuz you repented dear.

LATE LIFE ANOREXIA

MODERN TOXICITY

Late life onset anorexia in marriage: controlling your weight cuz you can't control your mate.

Anorexics: low attachment styles likely from alcoholic parents so marriage problems are serious.

Anorexics in marriage: low conflict resolution so she returns to the scales, her only solution.

Weak attachments, can't resolve conflicts: what else is there but to show power as a fasting lunatic?

When her one friend--her husband--acts up she loses weight then the marriage has bad fate.

When the marriage gets worse she falls into her bag of the weight loss curse: it's automatic sir.

She has no friends & can't resolve conflict: life is empty unless she finds God's love and quick.

SISTER ABUSE

Sister abuse: Something happens only once and they spread it around like it's a lifelong stunt.

Who else could ruin your life through gossip but a sister who's always mad about something else.

Latter days sister abuse: Who else uses you as a punching bag than someone who's close?

The dark side of being chosen is you won't fit in. In fact you gotta heal after being with them.

You gotta HEAL after high school from all that partyin' and fruitless attempts to fit in.

Chosen ones are left out of many situations but that's their chance to mature beyond em.

MODERN TOXICITY

When you're chosen the things you expected aren't going to happen. You gotta let go man.

You don't wanna lose friends, you want them to see what you see so inevitably they all end.

That's what "chosen" is: you let go & let God. Now you're going somewhere, free of the flawed.

After high school partying people veer off into their own paths. You gotta go with it, a lone empath.

Self-indulgence is a latter day sin. Are you willing to live some bad years for bigger rewards friend?

AFTER THE DARK IS LIGHT

After the dark you'll have light. But most avoid empty years with things only happening inside.

My "dry years" weren't about doing nothing. It's a fertile anarchy inside, truly building something.

It's a hideous image: being alone & friendless. But in avoiding the mess you'll be great I promise.

Some wanna get your attention and you reply back they say nothin'. It's for power advantage hon'.

Things like having the last word or ghosting you first. It's all about showing power and it's a curse.

When things go weird the first thing to ask is: who hurt you? Who were you around lately sis?

People wanna narcissistically abuse you and use mean tactics too. You must be ready dude.

Guys being abused by pretentious and deceptive females then everything they do fails.

MODERN TOXICITY

Getting back at the next person and robbing him because the previous person did you in.

Being robbed to "promote your book". Let it be your best lesson to not be taken by crooks.

Take joy in learning from painful lessons cuz obviously you didn't learn it before & needed it then.

Take joy in your friendless times alone, they'll put you on the throne. Love your pets and home.

BY NOT BEING STRAIGHT

By not being real, honest & straight with people you're more entrenched in the games of evil.

It's irrelevant things seem hopeless. You've repented and the Psalms says you'll win regardless.

It's irrelevant everyone else is in a ditch. You'll win in their midst if avoiding sins and the witch.

Lessons: you'll be robbed until you're not. A fool's easily separated from his money you nut.

Jesus said: "don't call me good. Only God is good." The heart is despicably wicked, that's truth dude.

THE FASTING EDICT FOR SUCCESS

Some sins only go out thru fasting. Is this your day, has God called you to maximum enjoying?

It's not just unnecessary weight gain but something in the offing. A new calling and feeling.

Success is here after years of hard work. You just need this extra push to put it all first.

MODERN TOXICITY

It's a very special day indeed. Don't screw it up, go forth into this glorious day of depriving the need.

The sin that only goes out thru fasting is obstruction number one: the habit of eating hon'.

Stop eating and your whole matrix changes. This is such a basic habit all of life re-arranges.

Everyone has days of blockage. It's time to fast and you'll love every minute of it, honest.

The fast is rewarded with insight & a hunch. Everything will illuminate just by skipping lunch.

SEE IT AS A SPECIAL DAY

You know it's a special day, you woke up knowing it ok? So give it an extra push by fasting: hurray.

They're a bad influence luring you to eat what they eat. Let it be a lesson so you never do it again see.

Get off computers and all other devices. Open yourself up to real life as eternity entices.

No excuses: this is the day you've waited for but it only bursts open if you fast for the future.

DESIGNATE FOODS

"Ice cream" is not made with dairy but with soybean oil. They're trying to kill us boys and girls.

Popcorn with butter is REAL. Ice cream isn't, it's made with soybean oil: it's a poisonous meal.

BACKSTABBING NEUROTICS

THEY WILL ALWAYS FAIL
TRAUMA BONDS FROM STRESS
HOLDING ON BY TERROR
TRAPPED BY A PSYCHOPATH
LIFE-RUINING MESSAGES
HE'S ALL ABOUT IMPERATIVES
YOU DEFINE YOURSELF
LEARN LESSON: LOCK DOOR
CONSTANTLY ON THE PROWL
BAD EVENTS WERE JUST LESSONS
THEY DON'T WANNA KNOW YOU
CONTRADICTIONS ARE TRIGGERS
CAREFULLY VET INVOLVEMENTS
ELDERING AND QUEENS
AVOID MORBID ACCUMULATION
THE INVERSION OF SYSTEMS
REACTIONS TO DIFFERENCES
MUSHROOM EFFECT
YOUNG ONCE, IMMATURE ALWAYS
VARIETY BRINGS GROWTH
THEY'RE OBLIVIOUS
IT'S SICKENING TO SEE THEM
ERA OF BROKEN MEN
BROKEN MEN & EXTROVERT ANTICS
CHEMISTRY OR TRUE VETTING?
MORALS OF A GENERATION OF MEN
FENCE AGAINST THE DENSE
UNFORGIVENESS KEEPS YOU ATTACHED
COMMUNIST SPIRIT
THEY WON'T LEAVE YOU ALONE
WATCH OUT FOR PEOPLE
INSULATE THEN CONNECT TO MIND
THE GAME OF GOSSIP
WOMEN LOVE TO HATE TARGETS
CONTAGION OF HATE
FRIENDLESS SEEMS HIDEOUS
MAD WOMEN REPORTING MEN
NON-ISSUES IN THE KNOW
MAD WOMEN REPORTING MEN

BACKSTABBING NEUROTICS

MUST HAVE A LOCKED GATE
WHITE PRIVILEGE SHOVE-DOWN
THE TRUMP DIVIDE
ONCE TARGETED THEY ALL GANG UP
REACH POINT OF NO RETURN
THE THIRD RATE BAN DEBATE
NO STRENGTH IN NUMBERS
VIGILANCE IS THE PRICE OF FREEDOM
THE SMART ARE SHUT OUT
WOMEN ON DRUGS AND VERY FAT
ECLIPSED BY OTHERS: FACEBOOK
OBAMACARE THE GIANT ROBBERY SYSTEM
UNIVERSITIES MAKE EM VOCAL/WOEFUL/BOASTFUL
UNITE THROUGH PRINCIPALS
RED FLAG WORDS: "SUSTAINABILITY"
AGE-OLD CONTRADICTION: CALL IT "NICE"
TOUGH LOVE IS JUST BEING MEAN
WOMEN BECAME DOMINANT
DON'T WASTE TIME ON USELESS DEBATE
WHEN JUDGES BECOME VILE, WICKED AND CROOKED
SOCIETIES DON'T LAST FOREVER
ADAPTING TO A SEA OF SHARKS
BRING IN THE FLOOD OF NEW VOTERS
CRAZY LEFTIST PROFESSORS
ANTIFA BEATS 'EM WITH NO-HATE SIGNS
FEMINISM ENCOURAGES DIVORCE
MENTAL IMMATURITY AND THE BANDWAGON
LIBERAL LOGIC: THE RESULTS ARE TRAGIC
FORCED COMPLIANCE MAKES FAKES
GROUPTHINK IS LIKE GETTING DRUNK
THE HIGHEST JOB IS HOMEMAKING
IT'S "IN" TO BE PUGNACIOUS AND RUDE
PURITANISM IS A RESPONSE TO CHAOS
THE YOUTH ARE ALL ABOUT LOOKS
TRUE EROTICISM IS SUBTLETY
ESCAPE BORING SENSELESS TRIVIA/CHATTER
TELLING THE TRUTH IS "HATEFUL"
DIET AND APPEARANCE
BURPING THE SUPPLEMENTS

BACKSTABBING NEUROTICS

To you sneaky little weasels: You know who you are. You thought we couldn't see through liars.

Please deal with these people with Your grace, justice, love and mercy so they'll be out of me.

THEY WILL ALWAYS FAIL

As you see the edifice of his false identity cracking and crumbling it can be humbling but relieving.

The narcissist is threatened by you being you. All the things making you distinct he will pooh pooh.

Those trauma bonded by a narcissist feel very self-limited and emotionally exhausted.

One feels unworthy after a relationship with a hyper controlling master manipulator type.

One can feel unworthy for decades without ever knowing it isn't them but the sick system.

Their malignant mannerisms show you who's in charge as they grind you into the ground so far.

You develop little belief in yourself as the narcissist fills you with them and fear of crossing their line.

TRAUMA BONDS FROM STRESS

With time you become so habituated to their game without peace a trauma bond develops ok.

Step up or out of his reign and you've had it ok but his limits get narrower with more constraints.

BACKSTABBING NEUROTICS

The following is what happens to a decent person trauma bonded to a narcissist for a season.

It helps to see abuse is exactly relative to your sinfulness so that's where you put the onus.

I asked God to deal with my enemies through his grace, justice, love and mercy til I was finally free.

HOLDING ON BY TERROR

They do everything to hold the relationship as if it's their job to keep the peace: terror without cease.

"Nothing and I mean nothing ever satisfied him. I had to be a yes person or face serious wrath, amen."

Lotsa verbal abuse and constant shame: calling you degrading names, never happy just games.

A lady said "I thought who the hell am I, and how did I get here?" She had to comply/hated it for sure.

Her worth and self-respect weren't just stolen they were trampled upon with deliberate put downs.

"To this day I struggle with doubt and profound grief." Through him comes the devil, the energy thief.

Another victim: "I feel like damaged goods--will I ever be acceptable and lovable? It's doubtful."

She is threatened repeatedly that leaving will end very badly. I planned my exit secretly/left silently.

A lady said "I felt so alone, the narcissist had everyone on his side & against me" in her own home.

Once she sees what she's dealing with she feels like a trapped animal exposed for the kill.

BACKSTABBING NEUROTICS

TRAPPED BY A PSYCHOPATH

The sick feeling of being trapped with a psychopath or sadist with nowhere to hide: beware sis.

Once I saw him for the creep he really was, how deeply evil his ways, I shut mouth/planned escape.

For there is no arguing with a narcissist and you'll only get dug in deeper with his resentments.

While planning I tried getting away from his toxic fumes but felt constantly terrified/sickened too.

An evil ambience gives me a stomach ache--that's the solar plexus yelling environmental danger ok.

This is what trauma bonding does to decent people--let it never happen again after meeting evil.

He has such a strong control agenda while thinking it's a reasonable thing to grind you, just a peon.

LIFE-RUINING MESSAGES

They give you so many messages robbing you of decency, to be bonded is a psychic emergency.

The narcissist wants to bond with you just like a python wants to slowly squeeze you to death too.

The narc is a mean animal seeking to bond with you thru trauma and toxicity--imagine such a thing.

He actually thought trauma would make me stay and after I left he begged me back to his den ok.

The victim is so damaged they actually try to protect the narcissist--"he's basically good" they insist.

BACKSTABBING NEUROTICS

Get this straight: he's disordered and pathological so stop excusing him and get on with it gal.

Drop the notion you're duty bound to the narcissist or anyone other than a boss/spouse/parents.

These notions were drilled in with Imperative Thinking: black and white or dogmatic "shoulds" see.

HE'S ALL ABOUT IMPERATIVES

Imperative: You must, you have to, you've got to, stick to the agenda & gotta meet deadlines too.

When they come at you with that heavy imperative it's a falsehood as all creative genius understood.

The malignant narcissist truly believe meanness bonds the victim because he's seen it so often.

Girl, it's necessary to claim your freedom cuz as water seeks its own level you're one down in the system.

They naturally suppose you're like their ilk and heap it on your back--you must confront all that.

The first shit test of a narcissist is to attack your notion that you get to choose for yourself: ouch.

He hates your freedom and divine right to choose for yourself and will attack it with stealth.

YOU DEFINE YOURSELF

You get to decide your traits or how you're defined but you may have to underscore that thru time.

Write out those traits as you define yourself including how you engage with people as natural.

BACKSTABBING NEUROTICS

YOU get to decide what your priorities are, not him. Your worldview too, routine, how time is spent.

Don't ever apologize for you being you, the narcissist wants you to get rid of values he pooh poohs.

After escaping a torture chamber it's important to have a confidant say they love you or they care.

I suddenly realized I was SUNK. That's cuz I didn't read the obvious signs to clear minds of a chump.

LEARN LESSON: LOCK DOOR

Don't let this happen to you. Don't get in a car, don't let him in and don't go in a home unchaperoned.

The trauma bonded person has been isolated. Find a confidant to connect with and gaze fixate.

Recovery from bonds of a malignant narcissist takes time so have patience-- take baths and naps.

Through a divine miracle I escaped and God rescued me many times from human sharks and snakes.

Who's falsely accusing you? The kings of the earth who gather together cuz they're weak as feathers.

There's something about the liberal mindset that if you're under it you feel crazy as it gets.

If not raised right by parents it's gonna be someone else and FAR worse so its best to learn it first.

A person into growth is introspective. What are the traits I need to keep and which to reject?

Narcissists don't have this actualization process. They do not grow and everything's for show.

BACKSTABBING NEUROTICS

Narcissism is constant insecurity--they're emotionally needy: what's my standing/where's my supply.

CONSTANTLY ON THE PROWL

Constantly on the prowl: what do you think of me, what will you do if I now change the status quo.

It's all about getting supply so he's very different in all contexts. "People do like me" he brags.

He lives behind a false self, constantly posturing to get supply with stealth but never real at all.

His anger is never constructive but bitterly reactive--snide jokes & ruinous innuendos intended.

They can chronically interrupt and hold grudges forever, it's hell being a target of narcissistic anger.

They criticize easily and won't let things go. Little things have em mad for days and months in a row.

In order to choose the highest and the good God had to show me the lowest and the hoods.

They insult you but recall they put our Lord and Savior down--Kings of the Earth vs. God's own.

BAD EVENTS WERE JUST LESSONS

Bad events were just you on the Potter's Wheel. Exposure to that level made you warm steel.

The anger is aggravatingly passive-aggressive: I won't do what you want, only on my terms: sick.

The callous have very low levels of empathy--a blank stare or questioning how you think see.

BACKSTABBING NEUROTICS

They make no attempt to know or understand you from the inside out--it's them not anyone else.

They forgot what you told them yesterday, they're just not sensitive to you save you aggravate.

There's no blending with anyone different from them it's get outa here with no attempt to understand.

THEY DON'T WANNA KNOW YOU

They don't wanna take the time to know you, that's how they operate. It's more get outa my way ok.

Narcissists commit to false superiority: a great deal of entitlement sprinkled with one-up comments.

"I just need you to go along with me cuz I'm the smart one in the room and don't forget it."

Narcissists won't accept input at basic levels. Another interpretation's enough to arouse the devil.
7
They always use denial: I didn't do that, you got that wrong, hell if it was my fault--you know the spiel.

They blameshift, tell lies and keep secrets keeping a very thick wall between them and us all.

You choose to live a life of introspection and the narcissist does not--so what, move on.

Things like defending yourself or explaining way beyond necessity may last awhile after that guy.

For years people may say "you've no need to apologize" because you're still in a mental trap, aye.

Signs of a trauma bond: a high control relationship with strong opinions but never any adjustments.

BACKSTABBING NEUROTICS

Its your job to fit inside their mold so they stress the notion of "agreement" and "adaptability".

Entitled, lacking empathy and exploitative while feeling superior--of all narc traits those are core.

A female narcissist will equally exhibit these core characteristics and cause as much damage.

CONTRADICTIONS ARE TRIGGERS

Most abuse is subtle--not obvious. Like hot and cold relationships you sense insincerity sis.

I sense insincerity and it's a mixed signal in me. Contradictions like that trigger acute sensitivity.

"Consciously I didn't question my frenemy but I was having panic attacks suddenly" said lady.

It's ABUSE when they lovebomb then minimize/discard or triangulate with another dam libtard.

How women fight: by inciting riots. That's the same as saying they get their flying monkeys on it.

They don't forget either/fill their cup with it. They're like shit on the shoe/you never get rid of it.

There is no kindness, mercy nor redemption with these masculinized women I'm afraid son.

I got rid of that boy/girl, he/she flaked out thru prayer and I feel like it's Easter/never been higher!

CAREFULLY VET INVOLVEMENTS

Carefully vet all involvements cuz it's like going down an evil rabbit hole once you open up to em.

BACKSTABBING NEUROTICS

California crime, criminal California: beautiful but trashy dystopia, sure can't say I miss ya'.

Retirement: not slow decline into sickness but before death increased perfection & genius.

In your own domain you've power to expel people. You are king and queen in your own household.

"False dichotomy" means they'll never have to explain why their position is correct/yours is wrong.

Due to virtue signallers we'll now have a much smaller piece of the   American pie and cursed.

ELDERING AND QUEENS

Why feel remorse for a mental illness? It was a result of trauma and you couldn't help it miss.

I'm photophobic, can't help it. I'm different every minute as a spirit but I prefer a portrait.

I'm different every minute as a spirit but the photo is permanent for the ages & I just hate that.

When I suddenly realized I was in control of my own domain as the queen the PTSD allayed.

I thoroughly resent any image of me unless it's a perfect portrait because it's permanent you see.

Do NOT blame your changed appearance on age except insofar as age means accumulation.

In most cases age means morbid accumulation: it's not pretty inside plus bloat from water retention.

But if you clarify the tissues--dismucus the whole system--you will surely retrieve your youth.

BACKSTABBING NEUROTICS

AVOID MORBID ACCUMULATION

Morbid accumulation of stuff, frenemies, anachronistic obligations, things holding you down.

You gotta control the rage or sublimate it somehow. I understand it but you must use caution.

Even outlandish insane behavior can be from trauma as the brain rewired and inner rage misfires.

It may take time to undo and heal from this problem but self-gentleness [e.g. naps] is the key son.

Anything new will cause a stir, bet on it. Anger, aggravation, blaming will be much of it.

His interest in you as a person doesn't go beyond his nose. You're supply, that's all he knows.

Anything new and they're likely to hate your guts. About humans I'm giving you the whats.

THE INVERSION OF SYSTEMS

The inversion of systems: You were down, now you're up. You were wrong, now you're right, the end.

An evil helper is a backstabbing witch. She feigns helpfulness just to destroy you sis.

Sorry to tell you this sis but the world's an evil place and you gotta be on the defense: get a fence.

You deserve to get away from callous, cruel, chaotic creeps and couch potatoes so common now.

REACTIONS TO DIFFERENCES

You see the truth about relationship when differences crop up, not with similarities nonstop.

BACKSTABBING NEUROTICS

Differences truly threatens a narcissist. Whatever it is they can't manage them in the least.

With differences they can't meet you in the middle, justifying anger/bullying against you, trouble.

In the midst of your unique differences they will **NOT** listen they will **ONLY** tell and that's final.

The biggest difference was I was conscientious and he wasn't, what sad days I had with that nut.

Narcissists are famous for drawing others into their dysfunctional ways with you/they're cruel.

She gets her flying monkeys to dislike you the same as she does, just cuz you're different sis.

They're also famous for stonewalling: killing you in the spirit as punishment for your differences see.

MUSHROOM EFFECT

You become the object of their derision and obstinance then a herd forms around it: social science.

Stand by your differences but also realize they're a threat to narcissists, so you set boundaries.

She was so dumbed down she hated every little difference in me. I had to release her to be free.

Your stipulations and assertive initiatives--boundaries--means just be what you're gonna be.

Eventually you see maintaining a relationship where differences are seen as awful is of no value.

Lowminds suspicious of anything different and in California that meant not-liberal/watch out.

BACKSTABBING NEUROTICS

Cruel, absolutely cruel cuz they think they're supposed to. Callous from inland deserts to coastal.

The hardest to forgive is their smear campaigns. Such a cowardly way to fight, for years it remains.

Primary psychopath reaches top of his profession while the secondary psychopath ends in prison.

Tho' rare the primary psychopath's success is unrestrained by empathy, machine like.

He was machinelike and unempathic but neat. Everything was orderly but he'd ridicule/cheat.

They make quasi commitments, feed a fantasy then leave you hanging by pulling back in duplicity.

It's called Evasion of Growth, also known as sitting on the fence. Say YAY or NAY the bible says.

Refusing to commit to a course of action he vacillates, hesitates then pulls back to old templates.

YOUNG ONCE, IMMATURE ALWAYS

You're only young once but you can always be immature. That describes all of human nature.

Weakness invites the wolves. Gotta be armed for peace then they leave you alone in droves.

To the guilt and shame that lasts long after repentance: I've had this, it's toxic/implanted/inherited.

When they're hot then cold, longwinded then silent, loving then apathetic, it's abuse.

Dead dry antiquated family trees they'll study but not you buddy you're just their granddaddy.

BACKSTABBING NEUROTICS

It was the smear campaigns. Cuz that's how women fight, unthinkingly, for supposed gains.

Leaving it all behind & heading for the sunrise. What a magic carpet feeling: all new/no more lies.

The cities are so dam disgusting no one even thinks of doing anything they just give up/don't see.

I've been smear campaigned and you're saying that's the right guy for me? They just don't see.

They know humans will adapt to anything if they have to so they keep pushing the envelope too.

VARIETY BRINGS GROWTH

Since variety is built into the human experience this relationship will only bring pain, a nuisance.

Time to move on to those who celebrate your uniqueness as opposed to stamping it out.

Accepting differences is a growth mode but not with narcissists: growth is only conformists.

Growth is not you conforming to me. It's we think differently so let's learn from each other see.

God said to relax after you do you work. Only would-be genius has an incapacity for leisure.

How can you live happy if scared every moment? You can't and finally see: nothing's worth it.

THEY'RE OBLIVIOUS

They're oblivious to how they're imposing on you so keep em out, live a high life, avoid coo coos.

BACKSTABBING NEUROTICS

It was the Dunning-Krugers who treated you that way. A whole generation can be dumbed down ok.

It wasn't your fault and you're lucky coming through it: relatively unscathed from a dangerous cage.

For the dumbed down are MEAN. They have the capacity for instant agreement on anything.

And they love beating the chosen scapegoat: man has two sides and evil is a bottomless hole.

You have been chosen as the vessel of hereditary guilt and shame, destroying every moment ok

IT'S SICKENING TO SEE THEM

I could see right through people and felt suddenly sick. I couldn't be the only one in this predicament.

Liberals have flights of fantasy then they flake out. They make plans but are rainless clouds.

The flaky, callous , entitled personality took over with liberalism making oldsters shirk them.

Hang with people at your level, not the dumb thinking they'll like you more, there's no way in hell.

Simultaneously illiteracy took over. Students watched movies in class and the teachers were losers.

Creepy kids we all had to deal with and for me that meant restraining orders: WARNING.

And for these reasons narcissistic sociopathy is the major personality of the 21st century.

They are losers having been distracted from normal development [childhood hobbies] by sex.

BACKSTABBING NEUROTICS

It's all a hundred year dumb-down plan through demoralization starting in kindergarten.

I'm whole, my value isn't based on their acceptance anymore. I don't have to feed my ego to soar.

ERA OF BROKEN MEN

It's the era of broken men with secrets to hide. Overcomplexity, treachery, appetites, blight.

They don't even know what decency is let alone to seek it. They have no lines just want to invade it.

Life is so simple now that creep ain't coming around anymore. A big black cloud/demons galore.

Because he's broken he leans heavily towards his ego in order to maintain an IMAGE of something.

Broken men hide behind alpha male rhetoric but honey you ain't gotta say that if you're really it.

Alpha males are quiet, they don't have to brag and make all that noise, they are certain of it.

An alpha male isn't suffering with low self-esteem to the point of compensatory projection see.

Broken men hide behind sexual superiority: "I've had it all". Come on dude that's insecurity pal.

BROKEN MEN & EXTROVERT ANTICS

Broken men use extrovert antics. Always gotta be seen, loud, center of attention, brash and bold.

It's a broken man trying to hide from the world with a smokescreen of fake behaviors seen.

BACKSTABBING NEUROTICS

A broken man is highly offended for nothing. Over supposed looks, slights or shunning.

He's always suspicious--"who you talkin' to?" He's passive aggressive/can be very malicious.

He's not gonna say what he really feels, just show you disfavor in other ways I'm here to tell.

If you're with a little man intimidated by your success and you ain't married him, release him now.

CHEMISTRY OR TRUE VETTING?

You have chemistry with him but you've not done your vetting and that's a very serious thing.

With a broken man you must diminish yourself to keep him happy. He can never celebrate you, sadly.

Mood swings, avoids deep conversation, can't express feelings, war stories of broken relationships.

A toxic man internalizes pain as he mutates to a sociopathic misogynistic predator: destroy her.

He's filled with anger. He hates the world, hates the woman, an angry nerd wants to destroy her.

Make no friendship with an angry man and with a furious man do not go. Proverbs 22: 24

A toxic man is unwilling to cover his woman--he'll throw her under the bus. Equal at first, now not.

He's not just merely broken, he's now poison. You're now his enemy just cuz you've risen.

When a man is toxic the first you see is his hatred for the woman, no longer covered by him.

BACKSTABBING NEUROTICS

A toxic person is always a mystery: from them comes a strange, crooked and angry energy.

A toxic, poisonous man has no ability to feel empathy no matter how bad you're hurting honey.

He's self-consumed but you never see that sis making relational decisions from the surface.

If still into looks, swag, brag--and you're not looking deep before you leap, your fall is steep.

Manage your virtue: your standards of who you are without negotiation or morals of men.

MORALS OF A GENERATION OF MEN

They voted for a centrist but instead they got a doormat who won't stand up to commie tyrants.

Americans feel insecure under Joe. Nothing is going right, we're losing fast, there's no food too.

The blue cities are dystopic mentally ill trash pits. They aren't just lunatics it's way below that.

She doesn't let a generation of men pull her out of her own moral standards-- and this is hard.

You must hold to your standards. If one, two, six or all walk away God bless em but that's how it is.

The schools screwed em up so they're all out of order. Mayhem, chaos, interruption, disorder.

They find fastidious order "uptight" and godly morals Victorian, stupid, a thief in the night.

If hooked thru chemistry but you haven't vetted these other things, be careful/watch out sweetie.

BACKSTABBING NEUROTICS

I hereby hand him over to you: one who won't be interested in a thing you say or do.

There's nothing more embarrassing than fake self-confidence. Give yourself a break: just be cognizant!

Most niceness is fake--they just want approval for the ego's sake. A plastic world is a constant dull ache.

Watch out for the guy who says he's for the poor but only hangs with the rich--he's married to a witch.

Always rising up as if he was gonna hit me, always asking for more money--that's a gigolo honey.

I recall as a child someone called me trash. It hurt deeply having been taught I was a child of God in fact.

You feel lasting guilt/remorse cuz you're a saint. The others couldn't care less/they're opaque.

When caught up in a shame spiral it helps to know it's not from our slimy selves but an OUTSIDE force.

By doing that you opened the door there. It changed you forever I fear. Watch all future actions dear.

FENCE AGAINST THE DENSE

Once system inversion [enantiodromia] occurs the gossipers must face themselves of course.

No complaining about your friend's grabbiness: just get bodyguards fenced from the herd your highness.

You'll have major problems not realizing the difference between you [the elect] and them, your hex.

There is ONE in the system who is MADE the scapegoat by repeated programming: "you are nothing".

BACKSTABBING NEUROTICS

Stop resenting nuisances in your life and start asking why you would ever let em in in the first place.

UNFORGIVENESS KEEPS YOU ATTACHED

Not forgiving em keeps you attached in your head while forgiving releases memory clots' instead.

A grudge doesn't hurt anyone else but me yet forgiving the thugs would make me free. It's just not easy.

I need a husband for protection, don't tell me I don't. It changes the whole equation/I'll love him a lot.

They don't have the maturity to know the implications of their actions and they listen to their friends.

What a revelation: all I had to do was get rid of him. Instead I kept taking it and it was so humiliating.

Who is causing trouble all over the world? YOUNG males and now also females, equally pugnacious.

This is what I mean by the communist spirit: if you don't share they'll go to war and they mean it.

COMMUNIST SPIRIT

Whatever I had, they wanted a cut of it. That's the communist spirit and it's awful/anti-capitalist.

It's not that our liberal friends are ignorant, but that they know so much that isn't so. Ronald Reagan

What we see are a buncha lunatics in America raging over felt slights to their ever-fluid dogma.

What they saw as a hillbilly shack I saw as ultra-historical and the only way I could get solitude in fact.

BACKSTABBING NEUROTICS

When I got married my frenemy instantly asked him for money. Whatever's mine ain't yours honey.

One frenemy was irritated my husband preferred me over her. The communist spirit is just plain weird.

God said forget the news: I want you ETERNAL not up and down cuz chaos/bedlam gives you the blues.

THEY WON'T LEAVE YOU ALONE

They scorned me for living "way out there" in a shack but it was the only darn way to escape their crap.

I'd be so happy when they'd leave and so blue when they'd arrive: in this state I couldn't thrive.

ANIMALS: I felt imposed on and robbed like they wanted a piece of me and everything else they could see.

What was I gonna say, "hey wait, I'm a genius don't you see? You just can't understand me."

They're all dumbed down as I lived with the Dunning-Kruger Effect of the dumb hating the Elect.

I ask two things of husband: Keep my head above water and keep people away so I can freely evolve.

They question everything you do. I tell you: stay away from me so I can dream/enjoy exotic views.

To husband: I'll see ya' tonight but the days I go SOLO which is a creative CORNUCOPIA when alone.

They're a black cloud/cloud without rain. They're a huge block, a disappointment either way.

Watch out for housekeepers. They're not just robots, they're listening in on everything/gossipers.

BACKSTABBING NEUROTICS

One housekeeper obviously catalogued my cosmetics and actually asked for some: the communist spirit.

Husband: Solve problems, keep my head above water and be my fence--now you can watch television.

A housekeeper started giving advice and I was so down I took it and our lives slid into hell in a minute.

WATCH OUT FOR PEOPLE

Watch out for drink, watch out for drugs and food but mostly my son watch out for people/fools.

The world says "leave home, GO OUT" while i say "the woman belongs in the home, never to roam"

Staying home is a wise adaptation to modernity but what I had to go through to discover the need for it.

NOTHING out there is as interesting and comforting as in here so don't pressure me that's my boundary.

When it comes to your wills, not a nickel to a liberal. Dems are the party of infanticide and criminals.

I'd be so happy listening to music, petting my animals and puttering then a big fat cloud would enter in.

Keep this in mind: The best saints were the worst sinners. That explains it all so ignore your mockers.

Never apologize for desiring to be alone. It's the throne--it's the highest you'll ever have known.

Being alone is an achievement of a very few. First you see the need but then you gotta fight for it too.

Aging should mean enjoyment of wisdom we've gained thru years but for narcissists it means lost suppliers.

BACKSTABBING NEUROTICS

They saw me as a worm so I went into isolation to learn, to garner energy for success in later years.

He's the first person you could talk to. But then there was disappointing aspects, there always is with you.

There is no reincarnation, I'm a Christian. But MIND is able to absorb it all, as if it was there back then.

INSULATE THEN CONNECT TO MIND

The more insulated we are from modern chaos the more we're connected to the Great Mind in all ages.

It's hard for them to accept we LOVE sugar and pile it on, seeing it as our fuel source/even our healing.

In wartime Poland the boy found a bag of sugar in the street. He took it home/ate like the elite.

Sugar is what they fear. But that's how we fill our glycogen stores and the rest is pissed out. Durianrider

I never saw anything so phony and classless but you actually thought you were impressive.

To stop thinking about recents I focus on history but then I see the exact same human currents, see?

Women love to hate certain types of women--the inconvenient ones, ganging up on the odd one.

THE GAME OF GOSSIP

Sue put me down to Mary who repeated it to Jane who told anyone who would listen: that's the game.

In short time every woman you meet hates you and you don't know why. It's the Female Community.

BACKSTABBING NEUROTICS

The Female Community is a massive obstruction to female genius. They do exist but many just relapse.

Females are really cruel when they want you to conform to them. The best nazi prison guards were women.

That is why the Bad Mother Archetype is so explosive in a nation of narcissist sadists destroyed by asses.

It's a fact women are mediocre thinkers save a few superiors. How else could they adapt to this?

How else could they suddenly turn on a friend cuz the balance of power subtly changed? Women

This is what happens when the man is no longer her head, let alone God who's replaced by paganism.

I became so absorbed in all these complexities I sought marriage as protection first: this was my reality.

WOMEN LOVE TO HATE TARGETS

Life in Poland: lowest was the Jews but Poles were a lower rung and German women slapped em around.

Given a target women really love to hate. I mean women REALLY get into it, spreading it thru the gates.

If they didn't have a hate target they'd be left to themselves and self-destructive devices.

If you're a target of hate they feel every right to shout your sins from the rooftops without any doubts.

They will repeat the most preposterous crimes and the worse the better for the women of the gutter.

The female genius ends up with no female friends and can't trust men either so it's God/none other.

BACKSTABBING NEUROTICS

As sisters put her down for differences it became a program of defiance/personality interference.

It's not that he treats you badly: you're the one hounding him like a mad lady, stop it and he's happy.

Women love to get in on the hate and will give up their day for it. Look at The View--they all eat it up.

Once they were a target the German women slapped the Polish ladies around. I recall this decades long.

Is female gossip/social collaboration a survival thing you think? Or are they just mean and rinky dink?

The women in town triggered toxic shame, compelling me to seek friendship with ruffians/frenemies.

CONTAGION OF HATE

It isn't that I did anything wrong to evoke shame but that I didn't fit THEM and shame's the result in women.

In a small town word gets around and soon every woman you meet hates you in this social jungle/zoo.

That's no way to live--daily facing hate--so the only answer in a small desert town is an old shack way out.

But then word gets out of your neat lifestyle way out there--and they come around, the same old scare.

Family said: "aren't you afraid way out here?" And I said: "No, it's in the cities and towns I'm scared".

You won't adapt to nor think like them--a stranger in a strange land ends in the concentration camp.

After the restraining order I lived like a monk for 20 years but then Jezebel Spirit entered causing tears.

BACKSTABBING NEUROTICS

Jezebel would obviously deride me to her male friends--flying monkeys coming against me in my own home.

I cut that off and Jezebel's gone for good. But now I have painful PTSD after all the crap she pulled.

You don't see all their traps and stunts at the time--these are revealed as you wake up later: shocking!

The stuff they did to you thinking you were down or you'd never make it. Or if you were friendless.

FRIENDLESS SEEMS HIDEOUS

I didn't make friends because I"m too busy in my head and besides there's no one who understood.

The whole culture is alien to me so I'm leaving soon, goodbye--but retiring to a mansion is a nice high.

You are way too social for me. So many people like that I've seen, they know all their names ya' see.

Somewhere along the way you were told you weren't good enough, ending in toxic shame/people pleasing.

Cindy knew every name in town but said she wasn't social. Yes she was, people were all she thought about.

Thru generations families build things to have toxic shame about: when it hits it smothers us with doubt.

Instead of praying for death, realize the trigger of the shame spiral--an outside force of the devil.

Toxic shame's not from something we did but an implant from another to dig our grave/make us impotent.

MAD WOMEN REPORTING MEN

BACKSTABBING NEUROTICS

Mad women report men for everything (false allegations). Guns, rape, abuse and other vindictive accusations.

A sick generation justifies it's addictions and calls it science. Of false teachers make NO allowance.

They're so evil this will be a turkey-shoot. The harvest is ripe for true evangelicals in their champion suit.

The kids couldn't be any more lewd. They're even proud of it so there's no debating they're crude, dude.

Stop following creeps. You are lowering yourself so much just cuz nerds don't get the perks.

In families and churches there are Jezebel splits. It easily happens cuz the brainwashed are sick.

They are not worthy of your interest. Stop following dense trendies cuz it reinforces your lowness.

Marriage is: A fence against the dense. You're rid of the stalkers and mockers--that's real defense.

NON-ISSUES IN THE KNOW

On and on they go with non-issues acting like they're in the know with my time to blow: fakes in a row.

These people actually think they're smart--yet they're dull, brittle, plastic and involved in black arts.

There are no boundaries with these people who want social tyranny but a locked gate averted the tragedy.

After my ancestors died I was the only Christian in the whole tribe.

Little people hang together but the smart stand alone (need body guards not friends to keep a throne).

BACKSTABBING NEUROTICS

Some groups have strict conformity (loyalty) and they ban autonomy (creativity) and it ain't for me.

MUST HAVE A LOCKED GATE

Just like a rich and famous person on their estate, no one questions why they have a locked gate.

Truth is eternal and unchanging but the herd narrative/matrix is infernal and deranging.
Few think independently, most go along with things unquestioningly.

They are so cruel about it, calling it "gibberish". These are sting-shots of the mean/mentally illiterate.

Let em see you as obsolete that relieves you of the mentally effete so now you can just concentrate.

People who are dumb have total control over you causing delirium but genius is bred in prisons.

We become what we focus on so stop following smiling trendies cuz you know it's all phony.

Stop worshipping people. It's a great evil cuz Jesus comes first or all you've accomplished topples.

Stay high--way above the multitudes who are dumb or rude. We're here to find God the highest dude.

Cuz they're too dumb to get it they blame you saying you're all wet but that's the human race I guess.

They are low-info low-IQ thugs driven by the thrill of violence, tribal hatred or whacked out on drugs.

Having such a limited vocabulary, when angry they resort to their bucket list: buck this, buck that.

Democrats meeting secretly cuz the "race narrative isn't working".

BACKSTABBING NEUROTICS

WHITE PRIVILEGE SHOVE-DOWN

I bought that whole line of white privilege and for decades even felt shame or like I was horribly guilty.

Non-whites were given mansions and every opportunity while us white folk were given shacks/ignobility.

Anyone they disagree with they call a hate group.

Some things never change and people wanna hold on to the rock of ages: drowning men call for Jesus.

Most everyone are two generations away from religious ancestors: it's in their DNA to remember.

America is moving back to biblical reality. What we went through to get here but it makes us so happy.

Why has Pelosi/Feinstein moved to the center so suddenly? Deriding Antifa when it was their baby.

The left is triggered by Harvey cuz it proves America isn't racist but hearty.

The vicious left says it's good the floods killed the nazis--aren't they sweet these violent sleaze.

I get such a kick outa Tucker Carlson: whether liberals or Muslims they never answer the question.

Calling us homophobic because we think children should be raised with both mother and father.

A small extremist community pushing to eliminate gender itself is not evolution it's desires of the self.

Rabid militant atheists are the gatekeepers of Wikipedia. Anything on Christ is deleted, no kidding ya

When I compare our great and loving president to apathetic Obama after a crisis it makes me sick!

BACKSTABBING NEUROTICS

THE TRUMP DIVIDE

The Trump divide: no figure has ever polarized so much but now we see em for what they are as such.

I am not black, I am an American. Trumpster

Don't feel bad cuz the effects of the sixties were disastrous: not realizing we were monstrous.
Obviously an omniscient God's plans are superior to mine, but the false church isn't the vine.

You were born for such a time as this. Your work comes out soon if you can just control their dis.

Nations repent and turn back from the brink. now they're back in sync and from peace won't shrink.

Knowing we have moral high ground is a magnet to angels. Moral certitude makes big changes.

White hair is supposed to indicate wisdom but the way old hippies act and think is without vision.

Alone: Once the bully finds you don't have social backing they attack daily with insults and bragging.

They encroach in a gradual process. It isn't all at once, that'd create a mess: just little bites of pests.

Eventually their ego is boring. Though narcissism is trendy I'd rather be soaring, so I'll be ignoring.

We can't wait, gotta do something now. The sky is falling and it won't stop till hell below.

All kinds of stuff happens when the devil is the default setting so why go back at all, no kidding.

BACKSTABBING NEUROTICS

The bible says we are not to mark up our bodies or piercings like the heathen do--is that you?

The victim wears his heart/hate on his sleeve. He's grieved but then their reaction makes him peeved.

ONCE TARGETED THEY ALL GANG UP

Once one is targeted they all gang up. That's the tyranny of the group so just close down and board up.

They hate him because everyone hates him. That's no reason--have your own mind, friends.

Once bullied, you're set-up for serial bullying. You reflect it all, made worse by constant worrying.

Witch hunts are always fueled by gossip. The herd is messed up: one hen talking to another--"wazzup?"

Half our world is men. So if they're being debased and wimped it's easy to devastate our land, again.

Don't race-bait me in this stinking con game. It's "white guilt" justifying all he does without blame.

The reason we've been losin' is our trance--we've been asleep. But now that spell's broken: we see the creeps.

Justice is what we want. We're sick of runts acting tough in evil haunts and thus this response.

THE THIRD RATE BAN DEBATE

Draw those lines. Against this terrible evil do your associates have spine? if not they're no friend of mine.

Is it wise to deal with disaster by becoming more licentious or should you repent and become pure?

BACKSTABBING NEUROTICS

If they ban, censure or shirk debate their thinking is third-rate. Tease out contradictions, take no bait.

Being accepted means you stand for nothing. The tyranny of the group bashes heroes who start bluffing.

Thinking they're smart they never study deeply but follow trends/shout slogans (having no heart).

You'd be shocked to see how they act when UR not around. When humans lose the crown, devils abound.

A chance to distinguish yourself from the living dead--it's more cosmic than any stories you've read.

REACH POINT OF NO RETURN

You reach a point of no return, sick of their tricks and false concern. Block them, say "no" then turn.

We had our hearts broken every day for eight long horrible years with a monster from hell.

You gotta buck up now: You have power-in-resistance and to that end I've given you the correct info.

Spring Break reflects an imploding society of mental illness. The solution to chaos is solitude: stillness.

Is this how your kids act? Spring break exposed: as low as it goes--so bad most remains undisclosed.

Spring Break shows how low kids go. They're like untrained children (chaos) yet still ducks in a row.

Trendies (fakes loving evil) have emptiness in their eyes. Conformists know nothing, they are the unwise.

It's not a democracy but an "authoritarian kleptocracy" and many of you went along with it, see?

BACKSTABBING NEUROTICS

Way to success: Totally remove yourself from the whole mess and then pray, you'll be blessed.

They call themselves animal lovers but post pictures that incite evil minds to do the same (they seek fame).

NO STRENGTH IN NUMBERS

They think: since they go along with the majority they'll be okay. Not true: you could die today.

The trendy culture is a legend to itself—a fantasyland. Like a boy dressing as a king though a con man.

They're actually surprised they lost. Though they be contrite we should throw the bums out at any cost.

For eight stressful years we were under the gun. With tyrants the unpredictability is evil and never fun.

He's had his boot on our neck for eight years and anyone who shined those boots felt many fears.

Men are being destroyed by feminists. Face this so they can come back to their duty to protect us.

It feels good to be proven right. And to be backed by the majority--we're high as a kite, outa the blight!

Speaking for liberty is the "animating contest" bringing out the True Self—the wealthy magic elf.

Tainted by rejecters, deny the tyranny of this group by eliminating the whole troop: Clean sweep then regroup.

It's deep thought not empty talk. Don't you get sick of trivia and fake smiles when beneath it's all rot?

VIGILANCE IS THE PRICE OF FREEDOM

The price of freedom is eternal vigilance. So said our Founders but we've

BACKSTABBING NEUROTICS

forgotten such brilliance.

The lamestream media won't report the truth. It's watered down or shifted: they are sycophants not sleuths.

It's all empty words: static that blocks inner worlds. It's hard to ignore but you must as God's preferred.

Pot lucks and patent leather shoes: It's not about that and sanctuary chatter gives me the blues.

The horrible things you see on TV: There oughta be a law--this stuff's so dangerous it shouldn't be free.

The most superior job is being a mother in the home and taking care of the house, not a lush and louse.

THE SMART ARE SHUT OUT

The smart are shut out in the bell-shaped curve--must know what's happening or you lose all your nerve.

True leaders shun the camera. They aren't doing selfies (that's just glamour) but good words and grammar.

Nothing's more powerful than addiction to people. Free of these blinders we see true reality with out evil.

Abusing men is the style. Women are coached how to belittle like the devil making him feel un-worthwhile.

They're fat and on drugs. They have a nice facade with hugs when going to their clubs but unplugged, they're thugs.

If you study deeply, you're scared. The dummies don't study then brag how they're "fearless" though unprepared.

The queen is sensitive to the divided attention of her subjects. Anything new or novel and she objects.

WOMEN ON DRUGS AND VERY FAT

BACKSTABBING NEUROTICS

The job of the older woman is to educate the youth on morality. Compare that to the broads today.

The New Tolerance says anything goes no matter how low. Think of that--in your own home, the foe.

If you condone bad things it's like you did it. Remember that cuz God's judgment is real against evil spirits.

If they're gonna act like then yes I will call em broads. Appalling, disgusting, freaky, odd.

They're on drugs and get fat: calling themselves "loving" and acting mature in chat but still just brats.

Go on facebook then get off of that thing. Don't go back for the whole day-- hear your heart sing!

ECLIPSED BY OTHERS: FACEBOOK

You can be eclipsed by another human even on facebook. That's where they own your reality, yuk!

They always show who they are--it's little things that make them the un-star. Rid evil and say "au revoir".

So excited now the revolution has occurred. People are optimistic--what a relief after hope deferred.

To them we're old and dead. Anyone past forty they're beginning to discredit so we all go PC instead.

What's gonna happen in the years he's got left? We're not outa the woods-- there's still death and theft.

Our only goal should be to stop B.O.: In doing so we're free again making money they can't blow.

The king is sensitive to the divided attention of his subjects. Those into self are the hated elects.

BACKSTABBING NEUROTICS

Please God give us a Renaissance--not going back into the radical agenda making no sense.

OBAMACARE THE GIANT ROBBERY SYSTEM

Obamacare is a giant robbery system. Raising taxes on poor people: the meanest law ever written.

They just wanna feel superior--everybody does. But notice--focus: are they not the real scuzz?

Operatives are stirring up riots all over the nation. They wanna bring in tyranny and then food rations.

The news is the fourth estate, a necessary check and balance, but this isn't the TV news--no chance.

They're destabilizing things across the states and it's all about race, precursory to Martial Law--disgrace.

Get a civil war going so they can confiscate guns and that's the plan for 2015 when the UN guys come.

People make an impact: you change your views/ignore the news. Stop, go inside, don't confide (no blues).

Normalcy bias, Stockholm Syndrome and learned helplessness are making us so much less blessed.

The music industry is a giant machine and they also own the prisons--as no-talents become stars risen.

After advertising for a hostess they were fined $5000 for not being "gender neurtral"--gov is brutal.

UNIVERSITIES MAKE EM VOCAL/WOEFUL/BOASTFUL

Leftist professors have way too much power--the major fetter bringing us down to the gutter.

BACKSTABBING NEUROTICS

It's true because it's true not because all believe it. Truth is not by majority rule or throwing a fit.

2/3 of college kids abandon their faith. Why is this? Because leftist professors have so much weight.

Kids go to college, naive and hopeful. They meet the creepy professor and become vocal, woeful, boastful.

Profs are a disgusting blight on these young blank slates. False weights, hell's gates, dire straights.

The restaurant was fined $5000 for advertising for a "hostess"--another feminist protest, no jest.

Haughtiness will be brought low: into the abyss. Social hypnotism is the biggest obstruction to bliss.

UNITE THROUGH PRINCIPALS

Unite the party through principals not ideas or politics. That's how you get all to agree on tactics.

It's a scary thing: Power and Means--If you give them they'll eventually use them (humans are fiends).

There's an epidemic of (false claims of) rape! From what they say and truth there's a huge gape.

Greenists/warmists are watermelons: green on outside, red on inside. Wake up--don't put logic aside.

We "dip" into things--crimes and karma. That's the best teacher but instead we resort to big pharma.

Why is socialism promoted by the most wealthy men? Because they want total control of all money, amen.

They lay an egg and then a bomb to divert our attention. It's a higher plan, man, than any election.

BACKSTABBING NEUROTICS

You'll have victory over armies with God on your side. Stay dauntless with obstacles and enjoy the ride.

To stop thugism from overtaking society, bring people back to God. This is modern slavery--bad though mod.

Since all men are sinners society must have order to contain it all so some can become winners.

RED FLAG WORDS: "SUSTAINABILITY"
Red flag words: Sustainability, intellectual, vegan, Stanford/Yale, global, gender neutral, racist.

They see tyranny as strong, purposeful and dynamic. What a crock justifying these things so tragic.

The best slave doesn't know he's a slave. That's y'all cuz you're the new wave but it's your grave.

Why do liberals hate: low taxes, freedom, property rights, prosperity or self-defense? Makes no sense.

Never trust wimps cuz they have much to prove. These were bullies in school so avoid them, I behoove.

The sixty's radicals though retired are replaced by worse guys saying it's all about regulation or race.

More division: Police brutality of black AND white is a disgrace--but the leftists say it's all about race.

They're right about mean cops but it's not about race. That's a set-up, a false diversion taking place.

It's a revival of reality--seeing good from evil. We've lost that distinction and it means great upheaval.

It's all vanity, futility and insatiety. The world is never enough--all we see is jocularity and forced gaiety.

They make up their own rules as they go along. This is not what the founders

BACKSTABBING NEUROTICS

meant to be strong.

Feeling superior, people can be cruel. They don't see you as a jewel but just a tool, that's the rule.

AGE-OLD CONTRADICTION: CALL IT "NICE"

The contradiction's as old as the hills: them acting nice but in truth they're mean, dull and empty in their vice.

While they disenfranchise one group they give a new one special status. From tension, take a hiatus.

How to win a war: recognize the foe. If you don't know that you're gonna die or eat crow.

Feminists advising divorce are just mad they're lonely and alone--they don't want you on the throne.

What you're looking for you won't find here. Cuz it's just a bunch of boring deadheads, not real seers.

It's not about race but cop's excessive use of force. But they'll race-bait to divert attention, of course.

He seems nice but underneath is a tiger waiting to come out. Watch out--he can even kill, no doubt.

They talk dirty to gain in popularity. But that shuts out angel investors who support goodness and clarity.

They focus on one thing and pound it to death then they divert to another to cover the first: sociopaths!

Human gangs oppress other humans--NOT about race. Whites too are killed/punched in the face.

Students are sick of (funded) race and gender baiting. It's all divide and conquer with freedoms fading.

Goodbye personal freedom, hello conformist clones. That's the way it is here

BACKSTABBING NEUROTICS

on out, says the drones.

Liberty isn't the fringe it's the whole thing. We should all be standing up for it, not keep reneging.

TOUGH LOVE IS JUST BEING MEAN

Called "tough love", it's just being mean. When the cold harridans rule the scene we feel SO demeaned.

Was it Roe vs. Wade that made everything give way? I think so---that was the immoral tidal wave.

80% of Americans are so against Obamacare. Defeat this thing or we'll be dead without a prayer.

Who wouldn't be scared we're going into total tyranny even in tiny towns though they still seem free.

Their goals: Racial divides with dumbed down public so social engineers can continue like alcoholics.

Do vegans care more about slaughtered pigs than human babies in the womb--can we assume?

Draw em out, see who they are then drop em on their head! This is war, they're the foe--now don't forget.

Twitter bans tiny slights by men about women but keeps angry feminist posts to "kill all men"?

WOMEN BECAME DOMINANT

Women became dominant just as men lost confidence. Build them up--make them cognizant!

Third Wave Feminism has nothing to do with equalizing and everything to do with social engineering.

Things of like tone vibrate together: the Law of Affinitization of Atoms (happy birds of a feather).

BACKSTABBING NEUROTICS

It's through oppression that we become strong. That makes it easier to accept when freedom's gone.

You wanna blame me but not the larger picture? You don't see them hiding the truth through vicious censure?

Angry women trigger anger and pets slaughtered. You don't like thinking so but ya oughta.

It's no longer a democracy but an authoritarian cleptocracy so stop your liberal humbug and hypocrisy.

What you saw wasn't Obama but a construct of those who created him: Evil elites made our future grim.

Why do you want high taxes, no property rights/privacy? Why do you want gov intrusion--lunacy?

Stop tellin' me to go to church if they're mostly fake. They've lost their fire, dumbed down for gov's sake.

Does the president watch TV all day, or does he have better things to do? See it this way, about you too.

DON'T WASTE TIME ON USELESS DEBATE

If you stop being a liberal give me a call. I'd love to get to know you better but if not we'll only brawl.

Failure of political will can not justify unconstitutional remedies! Forget votes, big gov is the enemy.

These wars cost 14 million dollars an hour for 13 years. Only 1% goes to vets and they don't care.

Wake-up! Why are you so dumbed down? City-water, flouride--what Hitler used to kill or de-crown.

Making us buy more insurance than we need for a price we can't afford--and for that he got an award?

BACKSTABBING NEUROTICS

Despite desperate attempts I fear nothing can be done. We're too far gone, they've armed and won.

Many women are angry cuz they think they're supposed to be. Where are the great little ladies?

Mindless tribalism is unfolding (the cops kill a black guy so now two whites have to die): how alarming.

There is nothing more cruel than a woman's wrath. See the female pugilism in schools--violence, no class.

I know how hard it is to see your world going to hell. It's really speeding up now, as far as I can tell.

It is disgusting what they're teaching your kids as young as five, seared consciences burned alive.

Societies going into ruin: they worship the carnal, a game of skin. It's youth-glorifying, filled with sin.

WHEN JUDGES BECOME VILE, WICKED AND CROOKED

There were many times in history where men's supreme courts became vile, wicked and very crooked.

What about what they teach children—to you that's all-okay? You don't care that kids are taught to be gay?

You liberals have made our world so bland. No cultural differences allowed now as all joy is canned.

Never trust supreme courts, they stink. Trust only the legislature--what we the people think.

The left can't think: Trump didn't say they're all rapists/murderers, but many are and it stinks.

Try to wake up family and friends. They turn a blind eye then call you crazy-- these are the trends.

BACKSTABBING NEUROTICS

Collectivism is nightmarish enslavement and ruination, so why'd you vote for him to rule our nation?

I wanted her approval my whole life--my rejecter. But now I see the phony social sister neglector.

Dear Father: Open the eyes of the people to see this evil then return to freedom, high as a steeple.

Any group will hold you down. Unless you rule you'll wear a frown as envy sees you as a clown.

SOCIETIES DON'T LAST FOREVER

Societies don't last forever. They prosper, get debauched then finally go into ruin--not too clever.

Medical Tyranny is where they force you into treatment. Painful chemo is cold, heartless and indecent.

I'm a moralist because I see the bad results from sin. They are terrible, weird, even fatal, amen?

I'm here to encourage you. I'm scared to death too and only a fool would think that's the wrong view.

"Take these BC pills and if they don't work get an abortion" feminists say, starting a holocaust, okay?

"Sustainable Development" is a buzz word of destruction--they're taking your land with out compunction.

The mark of true genius is sensitivity to conspiracy. You know they're talkin' bad about you, it's fishy.

I'm so sick of liberals--you've ruined the country. Look at Detroit and California you tax and spend mafia.

Where does it end--your acceptance of trends? How ridiculous must your complicity be, cool friends?

BACKSTABBING NEUROTICS

Trendies accept all things no matter how dirty, nasty, filthy or debauched. Sin is "in"--but ouch!

She is desperate for attention but that's not how she's made--people are so dismayed they need an aid.

Sickening sycophants: is that what we've become? If you condone their sin it's like you doing it, son.

See through all this evil emptiness and return to the real thing. It's decent and godly--not just a fling.

No matter when/where they lived, the saints transcended the culture they were in and repented of sin.

It's important that we take a break. This is just too much and our health's at stake with this heartache.

Realize what you've been through, taking all this in for eight years of evil through and through.

ADAPTING TO A SEA OF SHARKS

I live on a peaceful island in a sea of sharks. I must escape it now, having learned by hard knocks.

The biggest addiction is to people: an all-consuming trance which can justify everything evil.

Democrats are about destroying the old order. Sink the economy and create disorder.

To check for "likes" she rushed from work, got up in the night and had a PC in the bathroom: what gloom.

Was bored in churches all my life, all due to false doctrine: Lacking fire it engendered strife.

Until we see how bad we are we'll never see how good God is, ever. The "good" aren't that clever.

BACKSTABBING NEUROTICS

Until we see how bad we are we'll never see how good God IS--so get off your high horse, sis.

Have God-esteem (not self esteem) for God helps messed up people not you fakes supreme.

It's disgusting--the kids know nothing but that's the plan from the beginning: warp the youth by corrupting.

BRING IN THE FLOOD OF NEW VOTERS

We're in so much trouble. He's bringing in millions of democrat voters for a socialist bubble.

Take our guns, target patriots. That's Obama, Democrats and Hillary if she'd have gotten in--idiots.

Not ISIS but global warming was his thing. That liberals believe in climate change is astonishing.

Obama would've diversified all neighborhoods no matter what we want. Adapt or axed: we're just runts.

Lord please restore the dignity of all those degraded by the works of evil--in us and all God's people.

Brainwashing the weakminded is a powerful force by the democrats (the socialist Islamist farce).

CRAZY LEFTIST PROFESSORS

The crazy leftist professor said "looting is justified" and it's a 'victimless crime"--what slime.

The left marginalizes us (deflation) though these criminals hijacked our beautiful nation.

Chaos presents both danger and opportunity and that's why he loved creating it--not pretty.

BACKSTABBING NEUROTICS

It's not Anti-Christian to own a gun! It's just a tool to protect our God-given rights, amen!

"With too many words you give opportunity for misjudgment. Be terse: less is preferred"—kk

These boys should be working much, not going from house to house to deceive and mooch.

Dark upstart: When I say dark I'm referring to his spirit and if he's mean I sure fear it.

White liberal women bought the lie they're guilty and must atone through masochism: dumb and filthy.

Media rubs salt in our wounds, constantly putting down our past--no other country's past--and it's bad.

Liberals aren't well-doers with bleeding hearts, they just cause terrible troubles for the most part.

ANTIFA BEATS 'EM WITH NO-HATE SIGNS

Antifa beats people with "no hate" signs.

Stop hate by not attacking people with weapons that say "stop hate".

If one abuses you, the liberal will go on his side! it's weird virtue-signaling or feeling sorry for the snide.

Liberal females appear to have no sense of loyalty whatsoever, even loving your committed foes forever.

It's weird virtue-signaling of liberal females to like bad men, like that makes them a good Christian.

The more evil the man the more liberals will sympathize, feel sorry for, explain their past, excuses galore.

Revelation for the feminist nation: If you like bad people, you're bad.

BACKSTABBING NEUROTICS

He's so brilliant and shrewd. Trump said "you'll be so proud" and it's entirely true, we're wooed/awed.

False church and liberal females. Though seeming religious they're gabby, officious and hate males.

Feminism views marriage as a prison and wives as slaves. It tells women to wake up and escape!

Feminism says marriage is an exploitive, dishonorable, evil institution so you must get out now, women!

FEMINISM ENCOURAGES DIVORCE

Feminism says that all women should leave their husbands, no matter what. (feminist literature)

Family breakdown = hypersexual females, aggressive males. The two go together and it irritates like hell.

The feminists who say "heterosexual sex is rape" gets teaching posts and the highest salary rate.

Adaptive hypersexuality/aggression: means she gives up everything attracting a cold hearted man.

Sexual advertising of the self is called "empowerment" when it's really just setting the honey trap.

In war or family breakdown, obsession with looks becomes pathological (it's adaptively logical).

The secret to psychological success is high boundaries. Come within walls (KK health diaries).

Evil has a lure and that's why you're attracted to it dear.

The average person is so dumbed he's no smarter than a child. Yet question his beliefs, he gets riled.

BACKSTABBING NEUROTICS

They force divisions between friends. It's all so easy with the illiterate until everything offends.

It all seems good: social justice turning hearts to wood while they can't spell (don't think they should).

This is how they get us: smiley faces from an evil clown. Everything's in reverse, we're goin' down.

Jesus viewed the masses with great compassion. For it's sad what happens on earth, like depression.

Human urges, inclinations, appetites, tendencies, instincts, acculturated responses (all posers).

MENTAL IMMATURITY AND THE BANDWAGON

Immature kids get on any bandwagon easily manipulated, but you can change how life is fated.

Being old doesn't make you mature. If you're filled with clutter (not clarity) it's like an emotional blocker.

No matter what you must start lecturing about what they're doing to us. The harvest is ripe and stop the fuss.

The truth always brings offense. It's how it's presented which determines outcome with the dense.

With humans it's all about consensual validation of "reality". They negotiate the meaning of "normality".

They wanna believe they're all-ok so they avoid you at all costs, every day. They're scared, I'd say.

The hyper-sensitives are the ones degraded first. Great artists can see and thus fall under a curse.

Buzz words: racial and income "inequality". These are cues for takeover--you'll hear them constantly.

BACKSTABBING NEUROTICS

Once hypnotized it's near impossible to bring em back. We may have to hit bottom to return: fact.

The most basic division is male vs. female. De-gendering the bathrooms is the greatest upheaval.

There are two sides to the brain and the elites control it. Nice kids becoming evil and parents know it.

The saints feel everything deeply. We sense it when no one does, we detest the evil and creepy.

All kids need is bright colors to accept socialism then communism as our take-down abounds.

Women are getting pugnacious. A low trigger point, it's getting ridiculous. Feminism = lucicrous.

They're not happy, it's a closed system. No one's happy with out God--they just congratulate each other, man.

Even if it was your sister or brother, adapting to liberal logic divided you asunder—big blunder.

LIBERAL LOGIC: THE RESULTS ARE TRAGIC

Having been put down by liberal logic the results are tragic as they succumb to sins and magic.

The foolish shall shame the wise. Made fun of all your life I'll bet--that's the process, then the High Prize.

When due respect becomes dense disruption, kick em out for a genius can't suffer these interruptions.

There's endless variables determining what you need. Stop listening to others and from dogma be freed.

You should be far more careful of your associates. For it's an entry point to demons--ferocious.

BACKSTABBING NEUROTICS

The biggest addiction is people, messing with your mind. Things would work perfectly with out the blind.

Dear God make it happen: nemesis, showdown, whatever--pull thy lever to show he's not that clever.

Television is their weapon! Not only does it make men impotent it also deadens or makes them felons.

We're having devastating victories. Our work is NOT of none effect so keep talkin' to the Elect.

It's not "their" views, it's been drummed into them. They're pawns of globalists with silly sayings (not friends).

Isn't it strange how feminists put down all things feminine? They lack elegance, they are lemons.

FORCED COMPLIANCE MAKES FAKES

With forced compliance people become fakes--they're true image is shattered and they become flakes.

All my problems came from chaos--i.e. the TV. Plus the other victims of it always conflicting with me.

Though God doesn't need our defending, He still wants us to. He wants us to side against evil too.

Whether it be adultery or homosexuality, it's wrong. These main sins are recognized by all religions.

Every feminist has her own settings and threshhold limits of response beyond which she becomes a witch.

Make good use of your time by improving your mind. That's not Fox News (becoming a grind).

Golden Girl's Blanche brought down a whole generation of women becoming sluts, just like that.

BACKSTABBING NEUROTICS

The job of the older woman is to educate the youth on morality. Compare that to the broads of today.

Those against guns know nothing about human nature. It's evil--depraved--but through Jesus there's a future.

Stop being a heterophobe. That's what you are demeaning: godly family people across the globe.

Shut out evil spirits by not replying to ruthless critics. Love those nearest, only that has merits.

Consensus acts as judge and jury. But the truth is a majority of ONE, so forget these clowns/don't worry.

Blessed: suddenly you're a success, having gone way beyond this groupthink mess.

If you feel attacked your name besmirched it's the influence of groupthink as the left belched.

How dumb to think just cuz the others think it you're supposed to succumb to it. Be superior, dump it.

GROUPTHINK IS LIKE GETTING DRUNK

Groupthink is like getting drunk. This explains violent reactions when you speak truth and they're debunked.

Men: assumed guilty just by accusation alone. That's the influence of feminism and those old crones.

Gayness extends to pan-sexuality where anything with anyone goes. Perversion stems from it, you know.

You blocked them for a reason so maintain that line against those wrecking reputation.

The ramifications of redefining marriage are evil and infinite. Look at the consequences, idiots!

BACKSTABBING NEUROTICS

Tell a kid not to put beans in their nose and he'll do it. That's called a "bean job" so watch words, intuit.

True charm gets derailed by "what sells" and that's the false spirit bringing us down into this hell.

The most important thing evoking creativity is managing people.   For they hold you down and it's evil.

The truly creative don't flaunt it. No green hair/bizarre outfits--just do their work, not fake it.

They're not blind just greedy: in their lust for money they ignore it all even the freaky or cheesy.

The greatest job a woman can ever have is not having a job and just staying home, never to roam.

As you begin to know everything you'll face much opposition. That's always how it is, son.

Through Jesus the spell is broken of what other people think of you. Now you're untouchable, <whew>

The devil really is making them do it--coming in through entry points like media (should eschew it).

THE HIGHEST JOB IS HOMEMAKING

The highest job is homemaking and childrearing. That the fems denigrate this is so disappointing.

I just want solitude to think. But the social generation wants chaos and their thoughts are rinky-dink.

I was always studious and preferred being alone. The social generation hated me on that private throne.

Great thinkers separate from all they've been told. No gender or culture--just a part of His fold.

BACKSTABBING NEUROTICS

When people are given license to do whatever they want, the whole thing becomes a haunt.

They talk too much: habitually and idly. Whether or not they'll ever stop is very unlikely.

How has reverse logic taken over so quickly? Love is hate, freedom is slavery and people are prickly.

The happy homemaker got into the details of what makes life nice whether folding towels or spice.

All saints in history were persecuted. Loving sins, the heathen hate restraint and want us executed.

Why do so many white female preachers become "black"?   Have you ever thought of that?

Please God, kindly save us at this last minute! You've always shown up when good and evil split.

Because they're a bunch of selfish fools they don't care about the old folks they see as un-cool.

Polyandrous spirit: talking about "my men" like she's the queen bee. This will happen, like polygamy.

IT'S "IN" TO BE PUGNACIOUS AND RUDE

It's IN to dominate now: by pugnacious, rude, imperious females--even your sweet niece you should disallow.

The true lady makes homelife "pleasures evermore". Compare that to these culture wars (bores).

Girls accept this stuff as fact. it's all about demoting men and in that pursuit they lose all tact.

Women have become pugnacious. It makes me sad to see this carnal chaos-- they used to be gracious.

BACKSTABBING NEUROTICS

They're completely threatened by him--of course they are! His realness blows them to the floor.

Look at Madonna acting crazy for attention. All cuz she's getting older--it is beyond comprehension.

Just shut up about your "sexuality". Some things stay private and you never learned morality.

The godly must delete all rainbow friends. Take a stand, man--don't go along with trends.

We all have sins and there are many--but that's definitely one of them. It's not a superior trait, amen.

Liberals see heterosexuality as inferior.

"Is your heterosexuality the result of a neurotic fear of the same sex?" Listen to them, it's so ridiculous.

They make neuters of modern children by confusing them: "non-specific gender orientations".

Horrible PC culture attacks for committing wrongthink.

The left goes arrogant which always ends in ruin but in the interim it's hell living amongst em.

PURITANISM IS A RESPONSE TO CHAOS

Puritanism was a response to chaos. That's where the filthy mob rules and it's a disgrace (no payoff).

This isn't our end but the beginning. We'll all wake up and band together more, so just start chilling.

They wallow in lawlessness and gross perversions. Expect it and brace yourself but still give your sermons.

Tolerance was the ruin of Rome--but I'm still a mean bigot if worried about country and home?

BACKSTABBING NEUROTICS

You American women had it made: your men were nice and decent but all you did was bitterly complain.

The suppression of impulses was the fountain of creativity until the hippies came with perversity.

It's about the sensual. Having lost their minds they've been taken over with lust but still in denial.
What is a saint? He who loves God. Not perfect--we're all sinners--but he won't condone a fraud.

If they stand for nothing they'll fall for anything and that's the truth which is so bloody sickening.

Ok, enough complaining. Y'all know how I feel, that it's sickening--but I have God: the quickening.

Was he looking her up and down as she paraded around? Whose fault was that--it's a human pound.

It hurts and scares me so much seeing how most go along with this. A whole generation, dissed.

Stop all futile debate. They're thoroughly brainwashed--gotta be a better way to change their fate.

YOUTH ARE ALL ABOUT LOOKS

To the youth it's all about looks but what they fail to see behind the image is a bunch of kooks.

Stop being so nice. That's all just brainwashing as we're run over by enemies filled with vice.

Give me a break your thinking is so third-rate--it's good and right to judge or it's very bad fate.

Respect is precursory to love with males. But if they can't respect due to your sin, hit the trails.

BACKSTABBING NEUROTICS

He can't take life's bumps, he's got a short fuse. This Immaturity is always followed by an excuse.

He has no power on his own, it's all about lording it over you. He blocks your talk yet hasn't a clue.

Women had it so good before but now make life so hard as if that's liberation at it's core.

Feminism's taken over, not about women but destroying family and dividing us more than ever.

It's the style for women to hate men since the seventies. They aren't loving helpmeets but enemies.

TRUE EROTICISM IS SUBTLETY

True eroticism is subtlety but nowadays all we hear about is sex and it's really a bore, really.

When people had class things were so nice and women were respected and protected, alas.

It's her female indignation I didn't like. It's rather sickening, you know--women are supposed to stay high.

These ungrateful feminists need to know they NEED protection so kindly stop your bitchin'.

Lucy was always scheming against Ricky--spying has been fashionable since the fifties.

Sickening sycophants of the new world order, completely out of order while feeling so superior.

Using tragedy to push his gun agenda again, despite it being a gun-free zone that attracts em.

I don't wanna get into the details of the Titanic. I'm through with this--if I do it'll be my miss, gigantic.

BACKSTABBING NEUROTICS

It's not superior to be social--usually it's a waste of time. Best is an inner journey deep inside.

People impose their stuff and other friends on you. That's a terrible imposition on God's few.

Just shut up! You're talkin' way too much beatin' around the bush (so boring) while truth is snubbed.

According to bible the marriage happens when he goes into her tent. No license and it's decent.

Their writing is as boring as their talking. It's psychic littering and just noise in my system.

ESCAPE BORING SENSELESS TRIVIA/CHATTER

Escape boring, senseless trivia or chatter about sensual madness. Simplicity and silence brings gladness.

People talk way too much about nothing--trivia. The superior man avoids this, especially in the media.

The highest crime rates occur in gun-free zones. Government takes guns to push us off our thrones.

Government is force. Though local thugs come to get you it's still him behind the venue.

Culture degrades men: low energy levels, lethargy, fat gut--all due to estrogen/low testosterone.

The first rule of freedom is the right to self-defense. Even liberals find it sexy (just common sense).

Only slaves are disarmed--no free man would ever turn in his guns. It's about our freedoms hon.

We'll fundamentally transform it to the country it was. Our long nightmare of lawless bleakness will be over, alas.

BACKSTABBING NEUROTICS

Lord protect country from plans of a wicked elite. We're going down: sick, discouraged and effete.

Brace yourself for sudden shocks as people become more horrible every day. I Hate to say it, but hey...

The worse things get it's actually good for you cuz you reject early due to their false ideology.

Things are getting so bad it's like we've fallen off a cliff. It's full rush to death now, not just a drift.

And to think we could get stuck with Hillary, what tyranny--they'd come and get those wanting to be free.

How long will political agenda trump truth and reality? Worst scenario: maybe forever we'll be unfree.

Competition drives excellence, tyranny brings malfeasance and then crony capitalist allegiance.

The problem is not about race but police brutality per se. This is all part of growing tyranny.

TELLING THE TRUTH IS "HATEFUL"

In La-La land, telling the truth is "hateful". We're supposed to see everything as good, but it's hurtful.

One of the main sins has taken center stage as all the rage and I'm amazed how a Christian is hazed.

50 years of failed policies bringing poverty to the inner cities and now you want Hillary's fallacies?

This cancerous growth of redefining an institution which cannot be redefined means they die/fall behind.

One sin leads to all of the others and that's why we get picayune about it--sin brings down cultures.

BACKSTABBING NEUROTICS

Sunshine destroys political vampires so keep talking about these crooks to stop their evil empire.

Word of mouth drives issues in America so please tell all it's happening from the top: a world agenda.

In a land where everyone lies, the smarter ones go crazy--being most sensitive to contradiction they get hazy.

You get to a point where FOX is just noise! Good tidbits but the rest of the time chaos--we lose poise.

It can't be the truth if it hurts someone's feelings and the truth is what the group says it it is--really?

No one's safe in a police state. They can come for you or to the wrong address, no grievance addressed.

When success is based not on what you've done or got but escaping cops, we're in trouble--lots.

DEMOCRATS ARE SICK AND EVIL

Democrats are sick and evil (but then so are republicans) yet it's not about people but principals.

It's not just law officers but code enforcers--they all have swat teams too. Prepare, stay in twos.

Male and female is the most basic variable on earth. Blurred lines disgrace but it's all erased with rebirth.

Oppression Envy: In a culture where victim's are celebrated one lies by assuming an oppressed identity.

It is our constitutional God-given right to feel secure. But now even those in denial feel unconscious fear.

What if Patton said about WWII: he didn't have a strategy, leave it to chance, weather or cold apathy?

BACKSTABBING NEUROTICS

The anti-American liberals are aborting or going gay so maybe we could prevail in time, so pray.

How quickly our nation is deteriorating morally and that means judgment for a no-hope country.

DIET AND APPEARANCE

Feeling too full on salads or smoothie I opted for a piece of cheese: low volume but high fat/satiety.

Instead of a smoothie how about a beet chew--something like that/I hate fullness too.

Your new diet was a severe debasement on looks but you can get it all back, just switch back you kook.

They think it's manly to eat meat but it still causes glycation [roughneck] but not all show it.

Glycation: The carnivores who don't "show" it they trot out as an example of where you can go with it.

It's efficient to buy frozen fruit. There's no waste and it's great for smoothies. Get yourself extra freezers too.

Freezing fruit may kill the vitamins but not the sugar, that's still in there and that's our fuel source, ya hear?

Whenever you feel nauseous or sick, drop all supplements and add em back one at a time--it's them.

Supplements can give you a round moon face in reaction yet you can't pin it down? They're an ALIEN.

Hunger experienced as nausea indicates ulcer—fast for ten days and it's gone forever.

BURPING THE SUPPLEMENTS

BACKSTABBING NEUROTICS

Burping is from supplements if not food miscombining. All day and night long that's what I'm feeling.

Some take 100 supplements a day spending their entire morning swallowing/they're filled with powder.

They take green powders then when they do a cleanse a huge cylinder of GREEN POWDER comes out.

WHITE sugar or rice have near-zero glycation. You can put an inch of sugar on your cereal, it's ok man.

100 KAREN KELLOCK BOOKS

AFFINITY OR MISERY
AGELESS CORNUCOPIA
AMERICA AWAKE!
AMERICA'S DAFT ERA
ARTS OF PALEO FASTING
AUTOPHAGY ON CHEATERS
BACKSTABBING NEUROTICS
BETRAYAL TRAUMA
BOOMERS AND BROKENNESS
BOOT ON NECK
CHAMPION GUIDES
COMMIE NUTHOUSE
COMMIES
COMMUNIST SPIRIT
CONTAGION OF MADNESS
CONTAGIOUS MADNESS
CULTURE CLASH BASHED
DAFT LEFT
DAILY FASTARIAN
DAM RATS
DIVERSITY IS CRUELTY
E-RACE WHITE
EVIL FREAKS (Beyond Gross)
THE END OR A BEND?
FEMALE BULLIES AND FEMI-NAZIS
FEMALE CARNALITY
FEMALE DUMB DOWN
FEMALE POWER DRIVE
FEMINISM AND RUIN 1 & 2
FIX FOR MISFITS
FOOLS & TRAMPS
FREEDOM SPEAKING
FRENEMY ENABLER
FRENEMY LIAR
FRENEMY THIEF
FRENEMY TRAITOR
TRENEMY TYRANT
GENIUS IS HELD DOWN
GLOBALISLAM
GOD USES THE FLAWED
HAZE OF THE LATTER DAYS

THE HERD IN WORDS
HIX POLITIX
HOW THEY RUINED US
JUST SKIP DINNER
LE FEMME AND THE COMMUNIST SPIRIT
LIBERAL CHAOS & ROT
LIBERAL DOUBLETHINK
LIBERAL GALL 1 & 2
LIBERAL SHOVE-DOWNS
LOCK YOUR GATE
LOSERS and Femme Fatales
MANUAL FOR SUPERIOR MEN
MODERN ART FROM HELL
MOSTLY FAKE
NOTES TO CHAMPS 1 & 2
OVERCOME FRENEMIES
PC MAKES US CRAZY
PEOPLE ARE CRUEL
PEOPLE PROBLEMS 1 & 2
PERSECUTED GENIUIS
POLI-PSYCH MYSTERIES
PRETENTIOUS SLOBS
QUEEN BEE
RED NEW DEAL
RETURNING TO FIRST NATURE
SEASON OF TREASON
SEPARATE MEANS HOLY
SOCIAL HYPNOTISM
SOLITUDE SOLUTION
SUPERCILIOUS
THE SCHOOLS SCREWED EM UP
TOAD TO PRINCE
TRIALS CYCLES
TRUMP VS. GROUP
TRUST IN TRASH
THE TRUTH ABOUT PEOPLE
UNDERHEANDEDLY CLEVER
WALK TALL WITHIN WALLS
WE'RE NOT ALL ONE
WINNERS SKIP DINNER
WORK OR SMERK

KAREN KELLOCK PH.D.

M.S. Political Science, San Diego State. Ph.D. in Psychology, University of California Irvine. Postdoctoral: UCI School of Medicine, Dept. of Psychiatry [NIMH Grants]. Developed the Debris Theory of Disease, a theory of system pathology in 120 books and 22 textbooks for the general public. The theory has a general formula: All disease is obstruction, all recovery is elimination, all success is attraction. The three obstructions are people, habit and food. Remove obstruction and snap to your goals, waiting in the wings.